If This Is Treason, I Am Guilty

Allan A. Boesak

William B. Eerdmans Publishing Company
Grand Rapids, Michigan

Africa World Press
Trenton, New Jersey

This edition is based largely on the collection *Als dit verraad is ben ik schuldig* first published 1986 by Ten Have Publishers, Baarn, the Netherlands.

This English edition first published 1987 through special arrangement with Ten Have jointly by Wm. B. Eerdmans Publishing Co., 255 Jefferson Ave. SE, Grand Rapids, Mich. 49503, and Africa World Press, P.O. Box 1892, Trenton, N.J. 08608.

Library of Congress Cataloging-in-Publication Data:

Boesak, Allan Aubrey, 1946-
  If this is treason, I am guilty.

  1. South Africa—Race relations—Sermons.
2. Race relations—Religious aspects—Reformed Church—Sermons.
3. Reformed Church—Doctrine—Sermons.
4. Nederduitse Gereformeerde Sendingkerk in Suid-Afrika.
5. Reformed Church—Sermons.
6. Sermons, English. I. Title.
DT763.B553 1987   261.8'0968   87-15512

Eerdmans ISBN 0-8028-0251-6
Africa World ISBN 0-86543-055-1

54,215

Contents

Foreword

Nicholas Wolterstorff

Afrikaners are fond of lamenting that there aren't any true leaders among "their" blacks. The truth is that, throughout this century, the black people of South Africa have raised up a long succession of men and women with a courage, eloquence, insight, and vision of which any people anywhere would be proud: Luthuli, Sobukwe, Biko, Mandela, on and on. These leaders were almost all eventually silenced by jailing, murder, banning, or banishment. But the succession continues. One of those on whom the mantle now rests is Allan Boesak.

First and foremost, Boesak is a preacher, ordained in the Dutch Reformed Mission Church. He is also president of the World Alliance of Reformed Churches—an organization of some 70 million Protestants around the world—moderator of his own denomination, member of the executive committee of the South African Council of Churches, and one of the founders of the United Democratic Front. But he remains, first and foremost, a preacher.

He is a preacher of a sort, however, that we in North America hardly know anymore. Our prominent preachers see it as their calling to bless the establishment, at most muttering some mild criticisms of personal wrongdoing. Theirs is a theology of wealth, health, and power. In his prophetic courage and rhetorical eloquence Boesak stands, by contrast, in the line of the great preacher of Constantinople, John Chrysostom, who did not shrink from denouncing the empress in her presence. His reward was banishment. Boesak is fond of quoting the words of Kaj Munk, the Danish Lutheran pastor martyred in the Second World War: "What is our duty, brothers? Shall I say faith, hope, and love? Those are fine words. But I shall rather say: courage. No, that too is not challenging enough to be the whole truth. My dear brothers, in the service of our Lord, our calling today is: recklessness." What Kaj Munk was speaking of, says Boesak, "is the dauntlessness to stand up for

what is right, the holy wrath against injustice and inhumanity, the refusal to call a lie a truth, and the simple belief that constant obedience
leads to liberation. In our situation the church must also, with regard
to politics, and *especially* with regard to politics, have the kind of
courage to say what nobody any longer dares to say."

What is it that inspires in Allan Boesak this holy rage? Especially
two convictions, I would say. First, the conviction that Jesus Christ is
Lord of all life. "I believe with all my heart," he says, "that there is
not the slightest fraction of life that does not fall under the lordship of
Christ. Life is indivisible, as God is indivisible." And second, the conviction that evil is real and powerful in our world. "When we confront
the utter callousness of people who will do anything at all, destroy
anyone at all, simply to hold on to power, then you must understand
that evil is real. . . . Evil dresses itself up in black ties and black suits
and top hats, and sits in parliament and makes the laws that undermine
the dignity of the people of South Africa. Evil sits in parliament and
defends the cold-blooded murder of our leaders. Evil stands on the
pulpit and justifies the oppression and on-going violence of apartheid.
Evil sits in padded chairs in air-conditioned boardrooms, continues the
financing of apartheid, and self-righteously claims it is protecting the
poor. And in the meantime the prophets of God are silenced, not because we want to kill or destroy or hate, but because we preach a
message of peace, love, and justice."

The occasions on which these speeches were given reads like a grand
litany of the occasions over the past several years when the longings
of the South African blacks came to expression and were presented on
the world stage: the ninth and tenth anniversaries of the great Soweto
uprising of June 16, 1976; the thirtieth anniversary of the signing of
the Freedom Charter for South Africa on June 26, 1955; the meeting
of the World Alliance of Reformed Churches in Ottawa during August
1982; the meeting of the World Council of Churches in Vancouver
during July 1983; the Cradock funeral on July 20, 1985; the founding
of the United Democratic Front in August 1983; the meeting in Durban
in May 1983 to oppose elections for the new three-house parliament
(from which blacks are totally excluded, and in which Asiatics and
"coloreds" hold subservient roles). In addition, there are a number of
more personal speeches—though to speak of "personal" in this con-
nection is misleading, since all of Boesak's speeches are public occasions: the profoundly moving sermon Boesak preached immediately

after release from solitary confinement in prison; his answer to the charge by the minister of justice that he had committed treason; his speech upon accepting an honorary doctorate from Victoria College in Toronto.

Jesus once said that it was as hard for a rich person to enter the kingdom of heaven as for a camel to go through the eye of a needle. Biblical commentaries are filled with exegeses of this "difficult saying": that it wasn't really a needle, or that it wasn't really a camel. In the speech of Boesak, those who inhabit the underside of history find their voice: the poor, the threatened, the powerless, the shot-at, the tortured, the demeaned, the put-down, the grieving, the suffering, the exiled, the imprisoned, the outcasts. It is a voice of pain informed by profound and creative biblical insight. In this speech, one hears no attempt to "make" the Bible relevant. One hears, simply, its relevance. For us, well-to-do members of the core of our world-system, to hear that voice of pain and insight is to begin to see what Jesus must have meant.

1

He Made Us All, but . . .

Racism and the Reformed Tradition

Since its meeting in Nairobi in 1970, the World Alliance of Reformed Churches has not really given much attention to the issue of racism. Granted, it may have taken a deliberately low profile on this matter because of its desire to support the World Council of Churches in its efforts to combat racism. Or it may have wanted to give its member churches ample opportunity to give such support. It may have argued that duplication of such efforts is not necessary. Be this as it may, I am convinced that the time has come for the World Alliance to take a firm stand on the issue of racism, a stand which will be its own, based on its concern for and solidarity with those churches within its fellowship who suffer under racism, and based on its own understanding of the gospel and the Reformed tradition.

There are a number of reasons why I believe that the WARC should assume a more active role in the struggle against racism.

(a) The black thinker and activist W. E. B. Du Bois has been proven absolutely correct in his assertion that one of the central problems of the twentieth century is the race problem.

(b) The admirable work of the WCC in this regard for the last ten years or more has shown beyond doubt the insidious and extremely dangerous nature of racism.

(c) Instead of abating, racism has grown. Christians in Western Europe have become increasingly aware of the problem there, and in the United States racism has in numerous ways once more taken on a cloak of respectability.

(d) Racism has taken on new, more subtle forms and has found powerful allies in such ideologies as militarism, nationalism, and national security.

(e) In the political field, it seems as if "liberal politics" has come to the end of its solutions and its energy. The responsibility of the

---

This address was given in August 1982 at the meeting of the WARC in Ottawa.

church in such a situation is now greater than ever before, not only to challenge the myopic theologized patriotism of yet another brand of "evangelicalism," but to proclaim the vision of the kingdom of God, transcending the narrow boundaries of race and nationalism and bringing justice to the poor and oppressed.

(f) The last reason lies in the reality of the situation of the Republic of South Africa itself. Not only is South Africa the most blatantly racist country in the world, it is also the country where the church is most openly identified with the racism and oppression that exists in that society.

In 1980, black Christians made a statement in which this painful realization was put on record:

The churches to which we belong have conformed to the patterns of a racist society. The persistent cries of the black people that the church is not consistent with the demands of the gospel of Jesus Christ have fallen on deaf ears.[1]

Although this was said of *all* churches in South Africa, it remains true that the white Dutch Reformed churches must assume special responsibility for the situation. And since the work of the WCC has clearly not directly influenced these churches, the only truly ecumenical family that remains to utter the direct prophetic word is the WARC.

It must be said, however, that while black Christians in South Africa are almost unanimous in their acclaim and support for the actions of the WCC and to a lesser extent those of the Lutheran World Federation, the three million blacks in the member churches of the WARC remain painfully uncertain about the stand of their own confessional family. This is felt all the more acutely since it is the Reformed tradition which has been so effectively and ruthlessly used to justify white racism and white oppression in South Africa.

The struggle in South Africa is not merely against an evil ideology; it is against a pseudo-religious ideology which was born in and is still being justified out of the bosom of the Reformed churches. The importance of this for the future of the Christian church in South Africa is enormous, for ultimately, beyond denomination and tradition, the credibility of the gospel of Jesus Christ is at stake.

1. Statement by the black participants at the SACC Consultation on Racism, Feb. 1980 (published in a booklet under the same title, Johannesburg, 1980).

Racism Is Sin

It is not my intention here to join the current debate about the "right" definition of racism. Even while this debate is going on, the oppression of people on the basis of color, the dehumanization and suffering, the exploitation and rejection continue. The cries of anguish of the rejected children of God are far more articulate, and the suffering and pain far more real, than mere definitions will allow. Yet we need to have a precise idea of what we are talking about.

First of all, racism is an ideology of racial domination that incorporates beliefs in a particular race's cultural and/or inherent biological inferiority. It uses such beliefs to justify and prescribe unequal treatment of that group. In other words, racism is not merely attitudinal, it is structural. It is not merely a vague feeling of racial superiority, it is a system of *domination,* complete with the structures of domination— social, political, and economic. To put it another way: racism excludes groups on the basis of race or color. It is not only, however, exclusion on the basis of race, but exclusion for the purpose of subjugating or of maintaining subjugation. It is in this light that the current "changes" in South Africa's racial policies must be understood. The government, instead of bringing about fundamental changes that will secure meaningful participation, peace, and well-being for all, is making certain concessions that will do no more than allow a select group of blacks to have limited economic benefits and limited political participation under white control. The overall effect will not be to bring justice to all, but to strengthen white supremacy. In all these matters the church is called on to be particularly watchful and sensitive so that we acquire the ability to ask fundamental questions. Racism is an ideology that justifies white supremacy.

Second, racism has not always been with us. It is a fairly recent phenomenon that has become an essential part of a historical process of cultural, economic, political, and psychological domination. It manifests itself in all these areas. It is important to note that racism became essential to what Helmut Gollwitzer has called the "capitalistic revolution": "The revolution of the white, Christian, Protestant peoples that spread all over the world to open the era of slavery, which even today (albeit not in the same form) is not yet ended."[2] I note this to make the

2. Helmut Gollwitzer, "Zür Schwarzen Theologie," in *Evangelische Theologie,* 34 (Jan. 1974), 43-69.

point that racism cannot be understood in individual, personal terms only. It must be understood in its historical perspective and in its structural manifestations.

But, third, however important these observations may be, the Christian must say more. Racism is sin. It denies the creatureliness of others. It denies the truth that all human beings are made in the image of the Father of Jesus Christ. As a result, it not only denies the unity of all humankind, it also refuses to acknowledge that being in the image of God means having "dominion over the earth." Human beings were created in the image and likeness of God. In the Bible, "image" and "likeness" do not of course allude to any kind of *physical* likeness, but rather describe our unique relation to God. The likeness is not morphological but functional, dynamic.

The whole story of Genesis 1 and 2 is an attempt to give expression to this creaturely relatedness to God. The responsibility that flows from this relationship is "dominion over creation." This has not only to do with the source of this power—God—but also with those with whom we are to share this unique gift: our fellow human beings. At the same time, we are reminded in Genesis 2 that this "dominion" is *service,* that there is an interdependence between human beings and between human beings and creation. To have this dominion is to share this dominion— it is to be truly human. It means to be able to be, to live, in accordance with one's God-given humanity. It means to be able to realize this essential humanity in the social-historical world in which we all have responsibility.

To share in this dominion as a free person created by God enables human beings to become the subject of their humanity, to assume responsibility, to act responsibly and in acting to realize their own being and that of others. All this racism denies. It usurps this power to be truly human for one group only, and it justifies this action by placing the other on a sub-human level, not truly human, or not "equal," or "equal, but. . . ."

Racism is a form of idolatry in which the dominant group assumes for itself a status higher than the other, and through its political, military, and economic power seeks to play God in the lives of others. The history of white racism is full of examples of this.

Racism has brought dehumanization, undermined black personhood, destroyed the human-beingness of those who are called to be the children of God. It has caused those who are the image of the living God to despise themselves, for they cannot understand why it should be their very blackness that calls forth such hatred, such contempt, such wanton, terrible violence.

Most of all, racism denies the liberating, humanizing, reconciling work of Christ, the Promised One who has taken on human form, thereby reaffirming human worth in the sight of God. Through his life as a human being he has given flesh and blood to the words of the psalmist concerning the life of God's weak and needy people: "From oppression and violence he redeems their life; and precious is their blood in his sight" (Ps. 72:14).

Through his life, death, and resurrection he has reconciled people to God and to themselves, he has broken down the wall of partition and enmity, and so has become our peace (Eph. 2:14). He has brought us together in the one Lord, one faith, one baptism, one God who is the Father of us all (Eph. 4:5, 6).

Racism has not only contaminated human society, it has also defiled the body of Christ. And Christians and the church have provided the moral and theological justification for racism and human degradation.

Apartheid as Pseudo-Gospel

South African society is based on white racism maintained by violence and oppression. Legalized discrimination in all areas is a way of life. Apartheid means that in 1970 whites, only 17.8 percent of the population, received 71.9 percent of the national income, while blacks received 19.3 percent. It means that whites claim 87 percent of the land while 13 percent is "allotted" to black people. It means that blacks are denied any meaningful participation in the political decision-making process so that the process of "democracy" here has become a farce. It means a capitalist economic structure for which atrocities like the migrant labor system apparently are necessary, a system that, as South African economist Dr. Francis Wilson has pointed out:

can and does compel old people living amongst their friends and relatives in familiar surroundings, where they have spent their entire working lives, to endure resettlement in some distant place where they feel they have been cast off to die. This system can and does force a man who wants to build a house with his wife and children to live instead for all his working life in "bachelor" barracks, so far away from his loved ones that he sees them only briefly once a year, and his children grow up without his influence, regarding him as a stranger. One may close one's mind to these facts; one may dismiss them as being isolated casualties for the sake of a greater goal; but the harsh reality is that there are hundreds of thousands of people in South Africa who are cruelly affected in this way.[3]

Apartheid means that the most important thing about a person is not that he or she is a human being created in the image of God with inalienable rights, but his or her racial identity. It means that racial identity determines, with an overwhelming intensity, everything in a person's life. It means that hundreds of children must die—not only from hunger and malnutrition amidst South Africa's plenty, but shot down by riot police on the streets of our townships. But why go on? One should not pretend that the human suffering caused by this system can be described in words.

All of this is not unique. South Africa is not the only place in the world where oppression and exploitation are the daily bread of the poor and the defenseless. What *is* unique, however, is the role of the churches, more specifically, the Reformed churches. In a very important address given in 1980, D. P. Botha showed conclusively that the present policy of apartheid is essentially the missionary policy of the white Dutch Reformed churches. These churches not only provided a theological justification for this policy but also worked out, in considerable detail, the policy itself. It is these churches that from 1932 on sent delegation upon delegation to the government to get proposals for racial legislation accepted. It is these churches that worked hard to devise practical policies of apartheid that could be implemented by the government, while at the same time formulating a theological construction to justify the policy plans. It was these plans that the churches finally in 1947 presented to the National Party—which accepted them as a program that became a winner at the polls in 1948.[4]

It is no wonder therefore to find in a 1948 issue of the *Kerkbode,* the official mouthpiece of the DRC, the proud assertion: "As a Church, we have always worked purposefully for the separation of the races. In this regard apartheid can rightfully be called a Church policy."[5] In fact, as Botha says,

3. Francis Wilson, *Migrant Labour in South Africa* (Johannesburg, 1972), p. 189.

4. D. P. Botha, "Church and Kingdom in South Africa" (address to the SACC, May 1980).

5. *Die Kerkbode,* 22 Sept. 1948, pp. 664, 665.

The role of organizations like the FAK and the Broederbond fade into insignificance compared with the overwhelming role of the Church [the white DRC] in preparing the Afrikaner to accept and vote for a socio-political program that would revolutionize South African life.[6]

And this policy is "all-embracing, soteriologically loaded," complete with a theology to rationalize it. As such it has become a pseudo-gospel, challenging the very authority of the gospel in the lives of all in South Africa. The white Reformed churches in South Africa have not yet been able to repent, to correct their stand on the basis of a new understanding of the gospel. In spite of all the open human suffering, the violence necessary to maintain the system, the damage done to the church of Jesus Christ, apartheid still has their support. Our Reformed churches are divided on the basis of race and color, a situation that is defended as a truthful expression of the will of God and a true interpretation of the Reformed understanding of the church.

Within the Reformed family, racism has made it virtually impossible to share with one another that most significant act within the community of the faithful, that natural expression of the unity of the body of Christ, the Lord's Supper. And so white and black Reformed Christians miss the meaning of the sacrament which Calvin so much wanted to impress upon our minds:

Now, since he has only one body, of which he makes us all partakers, it is necessary that all of us also be made one body by such participation. . . . We shall benefit very much from the Sacrament if this thought is impressed and engraved upon our minds: that none of the brethren can be injured, despised, rejected, abused, or in any way offended by us, without at the same time, injuring, despising, and abusing Christ by the wrongs we do; that we cannot disagree with our brethren without at the same time disagreeing with Christ; that we cannot love Christ without loving him in the brethren.[7]

The Responsibility of the WARC

The World Alliance of Reformed Churches is a confessional family. The rationale for its existence, the *strength* of its existence, is the uniqueness and significance of the Reformed tradition and its contribution to the witness of the church of Jesus Christ in the world. It is

6. Botha, op. cit.

7. John Calvin, *Institutes of the Christian Religion,* trans. John T. McNeill (Philadelphia, 1960), book IV, chap. xvii, par. 38.

clear that it has a special responsibility in this particular situation. Since 1976 the crisis in South Africa has taken on frightening proportions. The events of 1980 have underscored this, and the blood of hundreds of children on the ground is a chilling reminder of the sacrifices needed to still the cravings of the Moloch that apartheid has become. Thus black Christians have said:

We realize that the racial situation in this country has reached a critical stage and that God is calling the Church as a liberating and reconciling community to identify itself with the oppressed and the poor in their struggle for the dignity which is theirs as human persons created in the image of the Triune God.[8]

The WARC has no less than ten member churches in South Africa. The great majority of them form the "oppressed and the poor" the statement talks about. They have a right to know what the Reformed tradition has to say about a situation like theirs. As far as the white member churches are concerned, they have direct responsibility and the power to change the situation fundamentally if they want to. They should be addressed in terms of that responsibility and in terms of the historical development of apartheid as it has been directed by the churches. The WARC should accept the challenge to address the meaning of an apartheid that has been undergirded by the gospel and presented as commensurate with the Reformed tradition.

The WARC should reaffirm that racism is a sin, reaffirm its support for the WCC, and encourage those member churches who are also members of the WCC to continue their prayerful support of the WCC program to combat racism.

With regard to the South African situation, the WARC should accept that it has a special responsibility. It should declare that apartheid, in the words of the 1978 Synod of the [black] Dutch Reformed Mission Church, is "irreconciliable with the Gospel of Jesus Christ." And, if this is true, and if apartheid is also a denial of the Reformed tradition, then apartheid should be declared a heresy that is to the everlasting shame of the church of Jesus Christ. To accept the Reformed confession is more than a formal acknowledgement of doctrine. Churches who accept the confession thereby commit themselves to show through their daily witness and service that the gospel has empowered them to live as the people of God. They also commit themselves to accept in their

8. Statement, op. cit.

worship and at the table of the Lord the brothers and the sisters who accept the same confession. Confessional subscription should lead to concrete manifestation in unity in worship and in working together at the common tasks of the church.

It is one thing when the rules and laws of unjust and oppressive governments make this difficult or impossible for the church. But it is quite another thing when churches willingly and purposely reject this unity for reasons of racial prejudice—as the white Reformed churches of South Africa have consistently done.

In South Africa, as I have noted, apartheid is not just a political ideology. Its very existence as a political policy has depended and still depends on the theological justification of certain member churches of the WARC. For Reformed churches, this situation should constitute a *status confessionis*. This means that churches should recognize that apartheid is a heresy, contrary to the gospel and inconsistent with the Reformed tradition, and consequently reject it as such.

I am not unaware that for the WARC this may become a difficult issue. But this is an issue too long deferred. It would be well to remember the words that Dietrich Bonhoeffer, a fearless partisan in the service of Jesus Christ, spoke to the ecumenical movement in a time not unlike that in South Africa today:

Not to act and not to take a stand, simply for fear of making a mistake, when others have to make infinitely more difficult decisions every day, seems to me to be almost a contradiction of love. . . . Too late (in our situation) means "never." If the ecumenical movement does not see this now and if there are none who are "violent to take heaven by force" (Matt. 11:12) then the ecumenical movement is no longer the Church, but a useless association for making fine speeches.[9]

Calvin's comment on 1 Corinthians 7:23 takes us to the heart of the matter:

We have been redeemed by Christ at so great a price as our redemption cost him, so that we should not enslave ourselves to the wicked desires of men— much less be subject to their impiety.[10]

9. Dietrich Bonhoeffer to Henriod of *Life and Work* in Geneva, 1930s, *Gesammelte Schriften, VI* (Munich, 1974), pp. 350ff.
10. Calvin, op. cit., book IV, chap. xx, par. 32.

2

Church and Politics

I thank the senate of Victoria University for bestowing this honor on me. I feel deeply humbled, and at once intensely grateful. In a real sense, it is not an honor for me only. I accept this honorary degree on behalf of all those who live bravely but without honor in my country. I accept it on behalf of those who are such faithful coworkers and without whose support I cannot do what I have been able to do. It is not so much me whom you honor, it is those millions for whom this token is a sign of support, of solidarity, and of faith in our struggle.

Political Choices and Deeds

My subject, church and politics, is a timely topic. Today, more than ever before, South Africans are thinking about the relationship between the church and politics. Although the witness of the church in the political arena in our country is not new, I daresay that never before has the churches' political responsibility been so pronounced or elicited such a response from the powers that be.

In Britain, church-state relations are strained because the Anglican Church refused to provide theological sanction for Britain's Falklands war and continues to ask some very critical questions with regard to its own role as state church in that country. In the United States, officials of the Reagan Administration fulminate against churches that have gone "soft" on communism, because of the churches' criticism of the defense policies of that administration. In West Germany, the German Democratic Republic, and the Netherlands, the churches' insistence on nuclear disarmament has caused the same tensions.

In my own country things are coming to a head, as can be seen in the Government Commission of Inquiry into the affairs of the South African Council of Churches. Some time ago, the South African police submitted to this commission a voluminous and most remarkable report

---

Allan Boesak delivered this address on May 12, 1983, upon receiving an honorary degree from Victoria University and Emmanuel College, Toronto.

on the SACC in which the council is accused of condoning violence and creating a climate for revolution. In regard to the report of the South African police, let me say this: that report reveals more about the South African police and about the government it serves than it does about the South African Council of Churches. Furthermore, the council is being accused of helping the victims of oppression, of giving legal aid to those charged in political trials, of helping the dependents of those who are banned or imprisoned on Robben Island or detained without trial, of helping black children to get an education. I want to say that we should actually be proud of these accusations. It is not a shame to be the voice of the voiceless and to struggle for justice for all of God's children in this land. It is not a shame to give support (even a few measly rands per month) to the families of those who are in prison. It is not a shame to help those charged under laws which should not have been on the statute books anyhow. It is not a shame when the church, in its own weakness, seeks to help the weak, the lonely, the dejected, the poor, and the destitute. And inasmuch as the council has been able to do that vicariously for all the churches, I say: Praise be to God! And I thank him that he has been able, in spite of our weaknesses, to use the churches in this way.

It is clear that in South Africa the church is on trial, and a careful reading of the report submitted by the South African police leaves no doubt that the church is indeed on trial. But I am absolutely certain in my mind that history will prove that it is not the church which is on trial, but rather South Africa and its government, and if they are put on the scales of eternal justice, it is they who will be found wanting.

But there are other examples: churches in South Africa have taken a clear stand on issues like conscientious objection, the presence of chaplains in the South African Defense Force, the civil war being fought on Namibia's border. There is the stand of the Roman Catholic Church on SWAPO and the situation in Namibia, and there is the Dutch Reformed Mission Church's declaration that apartheid is a heresy, with all that declaration's political and theological consequences.

So, on a worldwide scale, we find ourselves in the remarkable situation that while the church in countries like the U.S. and Britain is accused of not being violent enough, the church in our country is accused of instigating revolution. In truth, in all these instances the basic problem is the same. The church refuses to accept uncritically the policies laid down by a specific government. The remedy for these governments in each case seems to be to warn the church to keep out of politics and to stick to its real business, namely, to preach the gospel.

But there is more than just a little bit of hypocrisy involved here. President Reagan, for example, while running for office, made use quite unashamedly of large groups of conservative Christians and churches who helped him win the election. Then there was no thought of telling churches and Christians to keep out of politics. Now, however, when churches are resisting his policies and getting the support of many, the admonition returns.

In South Africa the situation is of course no different. One minister of the church does nothing else but engage in party politics. That creates no problem because he is in agreement with the government. Another minister, who publicly voices the criticism of the church against government policy, however, is immediately accused of "leaving the pulpit" to "dabble in politics." The point is: as long as the church agrees with whatever government policy may be, it can be as political as it likes. The moment the church becomes critical it is driven into the wilderness of esoterical spirituality.

But there is more to be said about this. In the past fifty-odd years of this century radical developments have taken place in the social, economic, and political fields. These changes are of such a nature that the socio-political issues have become increasingly inescapable. We gained a better understanding of the political reality and its human quality. We have learned that social and political structures are not unalterables given by God, but created by human beings and therefore changeable. In addition we have begun to realize the growing political responsibility of the church in general and of Christians in particular.

Furthermore, the church knows that its witness in the world cannot be curtailed by the warning to proclaim the "pure gospel." For what is pure gospel? It is surely the good news of the liberation of God in Jesus Christ for all humankind. But this salvation is the salvation of the whole person, not only the "soul" or "inner being." The Jesus Christ preached by the church became flesh, took on a human body, and came to live among people. His message of liberation is meant for the whole person, for people in all the aspects of their lives and their full human state.

There is another important issue, however. Some people feel that the church should be silent on controversial issues such as politics, for to speak out means to take sides. This argument forgets that silence can also imply condonement. More particularly: in a situation where there is a constant struggle for justice and human dignity and against structures promoting iniquity, neutrality is not possible. On the contrary, neutrality is the most revolting partisanship there is. It is to take the side of the powerful, of injustice, without accepting responsibility for it. This, it seems to me, is the worst kind of politics and the most reprehensible kind of "Christianity." When the situation is as clear and as unmistakable as it is in South Africa, and when the cry of the poor and miserable rises to God day and night and the injustice is there for all to see, it is unforgivable for Christians and churches to want to stay "neutral," to want to approach reality in a so-called "dialectic" way, and to find it apparently impossible to arrive unambiguously at the side of right and righteousness.

With all of this the situation is forcing us more and more to take politics seriously and to arrive at political choices and political deeds. But more of this later.

Church and Politics

Before we continue, we must endeavor to get some clarity about the terms we are using. What do we mean by the *church,* and what do we mean by *politics?* I hope the unavoidable brevity does not unduly distort. *The church* is the people of God, those who confess not only that they believe that God exists but also that in his Son Jesus Christ they have found new life, new meaning, and indeed have become a new creation. As such the church, the people of God, are strangers in this world, which means that they recognize that what this world has to offer, the structures of this world, the powers in this world, do not have the last and final binding force on their lives. They believe that there is more to life than what is readily seen and understood in the world.

They live for a kingdom which is not of this world. And yet, the church is the church *in* the world, and cannot escape it. It is *in* this world that the church must witness to God's kingdom and it is *in* this world that signs of God's kingdom must be erected.

Put very simply, *politics* is the ordering, the organization of the political, social, and economic life of people within a state, in order to create and maintain a society which is as meaningful, just, and humane as possible. To that end, a state needs government, laws, agreement among the people, and the consent of the people to be so governed.

14   *Allan A. Boesak*

Politics is therefore a very human business. It has to do with *people*. It has a profound influence on every aspect of people's lives. It determines to a large extent the presence of justice in society; it determines the measure of peace in the world; it determines the measure of human-beingness of people in a particular society. Because this is so, and because politics has to do with people who are created in the image of God—people for whom he has in mind a life full of meaning, abundance, joy; people for whom Jesus Christ had given his life—therefore politics is also, very much so, the business of the church.

The political responsibility of the church is to witness to God's demands for justice and peace, for a meaningful life for his people in the world. The vision of the prophet Isaiah is both God's demand for the present and an anticipation of what shall ultimately be reality in spite of the powers of the world who resist it. And it is a profoundly *political* vision:

There shall not be an infant that dies untimely . . . [my people] shall build houses and live in them, they will plant vineyards and eat their fruit. They will not build houses for others to live in, or plant and not eat the fruit. . . . Their labor shall not be in vain and the lives of their children shall not be destroyed. . . . (Isa. 65:20-24)

So for the church, politics is not only a reflection of what is but also a continuous struggle for what ought to be. Or to put it differently: politics is not only the art of the possible; for the Christian it is the expression of our belief that we expect the coming of the Lord.

In carrying out its political responsibility, the church is guided by the Word of God. This Word is the Word that gives life, and it cannot at the same time be the justification of that death which comes through oppression and inhumanity. It is the Word that speaks to our total human condition and offers salvation that is total and complete.

For us today this means that although the Bible is not a handbook for economics and politics, it nonetheless reveals all we need to know about God's will for the whole existence of human beings, including their spiritual, political, economic, or social well-being. The church believes that the Bible provides us with the fundamental principles of love, justice, and peace which we, in the making of our societies, ignore only at our peril. It is the Word of God which is the critique of all human actions and which holds before us the norms of the kingdom of God.

But there is another reality which reveals the inevitability of the church's involvement in politics, and that is the confession of the Lordship of Jesus Christ. Jesus Christ is Lord of *all* life, even in those areas where sinful and self-willed people will not recognize his Lordship. I believe with all my heart that there is not the slightest fraction of life that does not fall under the Lordship of Christ. Life is indivisible, as God is indivisible, and in all of life, both personal and public, in politics as in economics, in science and in art, in sport and in liturgy, the Christian seeks to serve the Lordship of Christ.

True piety never means withdrawal from the world. The tradition that I represent, the Reformed tradition, insists that Christians are *responsible* for this world. This tradition can therefore rightly be called a "world-forming" tradition. This means that we believe that this world and this history are given their shape by human beings, and we are therefore able to do things differently. More still: we *must* let the world become different. Carrying out this responsibility is not divorced from our discipleship of Jesus; on the contrary, it is a part of it.

In this fallen world, sinful humanity does not seek the honor of God and the good of the neighbor as a matter of course. It is therefore the task of the church and the Christian to take an active part in the shaping of structures so that justice will be done to our fellow human beings and the honor of God will be upheld. The church cannot accept sinful structures as if they come from God and nothing can be done about them. We are called, rather, to challenge human history, to shape, undermine, and change it until it conforms to the norms of the kingdom of God.

If the church does not concern itself sufficiently with justice, with peace, with love and reconciliation, or, more concretely, with the very poor, the wronged and oppressed, it disobeys the Lord and denies the "good news." The church must therefore be tested, not only on the scriptural basis of its doctrine, but also on the outcome of its diaconal calling and most certainly also on the evidence of its socio-political compassion. For the church is not an end in itself, but a means to be used by God in the world. And the service of the church to God will be known by its service in and to the world.

Freedom and Partiality

We believe we have now made it clear that the church has no choice: it has a particular political responsibility. It must speak. Sometimes its utterances will be more pastoral, where it concerns a matter not requiring an immediate decision, or where the general opinions are so diverse that the church can only gradually guide the people to a decision. Sometimes the church will have to speak in a prophetic, admonishing way, even judgmentally, especially if there is much at stake, even for just *one* person: life or death, freedom or bondage, the integrity of the church or the credibility of the gospel. Apartheid is an example of the latter. The church finds the entire ideology with all its practical implications so much in conflict with the fundamental principles of the gospel that no other language is permitted here.

This can cause tension within the church. The church will quite rightly have to guard against rashness and will have to give deliberate polarization no quarter. But it is unrealistic to think that all church members will be satisfied with the church's work toward changing political, economic, and social power structures. Those who think that a more equitable distribution of wealth will upset their privileges will never be satisfied with fundamental changes. The same applies to political equalization. The church will have to guard against having the quality of its involvement determined by the members with the greatest influence and status. The church will, instead, have to apply the criterion of Scripture, namely the test of "the least of the brothers and sisters. . . ."

The church will also have to treat with care the very admonition to be "careful." We should like, in this context, to call to mind the famous words of the Reverend Kaj Munk, that Christian hero of Denmark who, in the midst of the German occupation of his country in 1943, reminded his fellow clergy that the symbols of the church had always been the lion, the lamb, the fish, and the dove, but *never* the chameleon. And when the church was cautioned to be careful in view of the difficulty of the situation (the Germans were merciless, after all, and many members of the church were sympathetic to the Nazis) Kaj Munk ended an address on "The Calling of the Preacher Today" with the words: "What is our duty, brothers? Shall I say faith, hope, and love? Those are fine words. But I shall rather say: courage. No, that too is not challenging enough to be the *whole* truth. My dear brothers in the service of the Lord, our calling today is: recklessness."

What Kaj Munk speaks of is the dauntlessness to stand up for what is right, the holy wrath against injustice and inhumanity, the refusal to call a lie a truth, and the simple belief that constant obedience leads to liberation.

In our situation the church must also, with regard to politics, and *especially* with regard to politics, have the kind of courage to say what nobody any longer dares to say.

In saying all of this, I must emphasize that the gospel is free and not to be identified with any party ideology. For this reason the church should not become servant to any party or any ideological grouping. It must retain its critical distance simply because its loyalty is not to any party or grouping, but ultimately to the Lord and his kingdom.

Nonetheless that same gospel calls for clear choices. The God of the Bible is a God of such clear choices. He is called the God of the poor (Pss. 72, 82, 146) because he stands on the side of the poor, the oppressed, and the downtrodden. The church has no other option but to follow her Lord in this. This means that the church will have to make concrete political decisions and make clear political choices.

It is possible, therefore, that the church, while rejecting the policy of a particular political party on a specific issue, may have to support another party whose policy on that specific issue is more in accord with the criteria the church has to apply. In doing this the church does not surrender itself to the party—the choice is an *ad hoc* one, for a specific moment and on a specific issue. What is at stake here is not a blanket divine sanction for the party as party, but the legitimacy of a specific, important issue on which this particular party had taken the right stand in the judgment of the church. This is indeed the sharp edge of the knife and here the church must move with delicate sensitivity.

Many have said that the churches in South Africa, in taking the clear stand that they have with regard to the government's constitutional proposals, have embroiled themselves in party politics. In terms of our reasoning until now, we must reject that claim. But we must reject it also in terms of this particular issue itself.

The church, not bound by the ethnic parameters laid down by the government and speaking therefore for its members across the color lines drawn by the government, finds itself, in its opposition to the government, opposed by an ethnic political party. Does that make the church's stance a party-political one? The answer must surely be *no*. Moreover, the churches' opposition to these new proposals is consistently in line with the churches' stand on apartheid. The churches are convinced that these new proposals do not represent meaningful change away from apartheid, but rather an entrenchment of apartheid. It gives the system more elasticity which a) gives the system a longer lease on life; b) makes meaningful change even more difficult; and c) exacerbates the already volatile situation in which we find ourselves.

Therefore, the churches are opposing the same basic ideology (albeit with a new multicolored face) that they have been opposing for so long. To take an example from my own church, the Dutch Reformed Mission Church. Synod decisions from 1978 and 1982 affirm that apartheid is contrary to the gospel—the 1982 synod speaks of "heresy" and "idolatry." Synod speaks of the demand of the gospel that "justice be done to all [South Africa's people]." A report to the 1982 synod asks for "meaningful participation in a democratic process of decision making and consultation" and judged it "in accord with the biblical demand for justice." In this process, "no population group shall be excluded. . . ."

But the D. R. Mission Church went further. It adopted a proposed confession with more than ecclesiastical consequences. This confession not only rejects emphatically the separation of people on ethnic grounds but also states boldly that the church ought to be on the side of those who suffer injustice and oppression. The confession says: "We believe that God . . . is in a special way the God of the destitute, the poor and the wronged and that He calls His church to follow Him in this; . . . that the church as the possession of God must stand where He stands, namely against injustice and with the wronged; that in following Christ the church must witness against the powerful and privileged who selfishly seek to control and harm others."

In the new constitutional proposals, the enforced separation of people on ethnic grounds, the exclusion of others from meaningful participation, continue. Clearly, the injustices are being perpetuated. The line of exclusion is not eradicated but simply shifted.

So-called "colored" and "Indians" are being incorporated into the privileged (white) class "who selfishly seek their own interests and seek to control and harm others" as the confession says. Therefore, the D. R. Mission Church has no option. In terms of its own principled reasoning, its own theological convictions, it has to say "no" to these proposals. And it has indeed done so. I submit that this is not a party-political stand, but a stand based on the understanding of the church of the demands of the gospel. We are saying nothing new: we are simply affirming a broad ecumenical consensus.

Of course one may ask if such an explicit attitude does not jeopardize the unity of the church, as some have indeed suggested. I think that that is a legitimate concern. But in the church our concern is not only the *unity within* the church but also the *truth* without which the church cannot live. We are concerned not only about the *common mind* of the church but even more about the *faithful obedience* to the Lord of the church. If the unity of the church is not built upon the passion for truth, the desire for justice, the faithful obedience to the Lord whatever the cost, then it is no unity at all.

And it is well that we are reminded of the words of Bullinger, the young successor to Ulrich Zwingli in Zurich. The city council, after being disturbed by the political pronunciations of the young preacher, had issued the famous Article Four, which stated that the city should call only ministers who were "men of peace." Furthermore, the city would allow no interference with politics, but "you must leave us to govern . . . in as Christian a fashion as we can, according to what would be advantageous for our country." In response, Bullinger reminded them of the political content of the Bible itself and went on to say, "We do not have the authority to withdraw the Word of God from anything at all in this world."

Oh, for a church today that would be as forthright, as simple, as clear, as faithful.

In this, as in all matters, it remains true: the church is the chosen people of God. Many are called, but few are chosen. And the chosen shall be known by their choices.

3

A Christian Response to the New Constitution

The churches have to remain clear and unambiguous in our opposition to the new constitutional proposals for several reasons. The preamble to these new proposals states that the constitution seeks "to uphold Christian standards" in South Africa. We are led to believe that that assertion is based on the fact that this country wants to be a "Christian" country, and that its government wants to be known as a "Christian" government. That also implies that the government knows and understands the commandments of the God of the Bible in terms of justice, peace, and human liberation, and that what the government does is to govern in such a way that these goals are realized and that the glory of God is served. There is of course the further implication that such a "Christian" government should have the full support of the Christian church.

But let us for the moment concentrate on what the government considers to be the "Christian standards" it is called to uphold through the implementation of the new proposals. Among these Christian standards, we are told, are:

—the integrity and freedom of the country
—the maintenance of law and order
—an independent judiciary
—private enterprise
—the duty to seek world peace

Apart from the important question why the government should choose to ignore the pluriform nature of our South African society—after all, how should a good Moslem or a dedicated Hindu cooperate in uphold-

The government's proposed new constitution called for a three-house parliament, composed of white, mixed-race "colored," and Asian (Indian) segments. Allan Boesak delivered this reaction in Durban on May 21, 1983.

ing Christian standards?—there is another question. Should our Christian standards be forced down the throats of those who do not adhere to Christianity? Should we not rather live in such a way that others are attracted to the church and to the gospel, not because it will be politically advantageous, but because the witness, the lifestyle, the courage and faithfulness of Christians will be such that others will ask: "Who is this Jesus whom you proclaim?"

But still another question remains, namely, what is "Christian" in what the government is trying to do? Something is not Christian simply because a government declares it so. Rather it is Christian because it is in accord with the demands of the gospel of Jesus the Messiah. The Christian church in South Africa must not be intimidated or brainwashed by propaganda in our efforts to discern what is Christian or not. We are called, rather, to test the spirits, and to apply the criteria of the kingdom of God—justice, love, peace, reconciliation—in this process of discernment. And these are the criteria we will apply in judging whether the constitutional proposals are in accord with the gospel or not.

Let us therefore look at these "Christian aims" in the proposed constitution a little more closely. And in doing so we must look not only at the terminology used but also at the context within which it is used.

We must, as Christians, the constitution says, preserve the integrity and freedom of our country. But already here the questions abound. What is freedom? And who is free in South Africa—in other words, whose freedom must be defended? In what lies the integrity of our country? Does it not lie in the freedom of all its children, in the diligent pursuit of justice, in the recognition and faithful defense of the human dignity of all? Does it not lie in the fact that the practices and policies of the government are commensurate with the lofty ideals that it claims? Does a land have integrity when it destroys, systematically and by design, the human dignity of its citizens, when it makes as irrelevant and fickle a thing as racial identity the key to the understanding of human relationships, political participation, and economic justice? Does it have integrity when in the name of Christianity it pursues policies which cause little children to die of hunger and malnutrition, which break up black family life, and which spell out a continuous hopeless death for millions of black people?

The vast majority of South Africa's people are *not* free—that is true. But neither are the whites, who think that their security and peace lie in the perpetuation of intimidation, dehumanization, and violence. They will never be free as long as they have to kill our children in order to safeguard their over-privileged positions. They will never be free as long as they have to lie awake at night worrying whether a black government will one day do the same to them as they are doing to us, when white power will have come to its inevitable end.

One has to presume that the country's integrity and freedom have to be defended against "the communists." We have no reason to laud the communists, but we must not blame them for things they did not do. It was not the communists who took away our land, who created the homelands, who drafted the security legislation, who detain those who struggle for justice without trial, torturing them in the jails and banning them into virtual nonexistence. It is not the communists who have created the group areas act and have therefore legally robbed millions of people of their homes. It is not the communists who have killed Steve Biko and Saul Mkhize. So while the communists have a lot to answer for, these things that have happened in this country they did not do. These are done by the South African government that claims to be Christian and that wants us to accept the new constitution because it claims to be a "Christian" constitution. No, whatever the communists have done, and God knows their misdeeds are many, they have not done them in the name of our Lord and Savior Jesus Christ. Therefore God's judgment shall be harsher on this government because it, knowing the Name above all names, has deliberately and consistently profaned it. Therefore the churches, as deliberately and consistently, must remind the government: "You shall not take the name of the Lord your God in vain!" And "you shall reap what you sow!"

And what shall we say about law and order as a Christian aim? Does the government mean the racist laws that have become the hallmark of this country? The Group Areas Act, or the Pass Laws, the Mixed Marriages Act, or any of the other discriminatory laws which are designed to secure white people's whiteness and their privileged position? Does the constitution speak about the so-called security laws, maybe? Is detention without trial, unexplained deaths in detention, and torture a Christian form of law and order? Is Christian law and order killing of children on the streets who protest against apartheid and its evils? No, a thousand times No! The church cannot accept that. We must be clear in our witness that this kind of law and order is in fact a travesty of justice. The people are not there for the law, but the law, like the Sabbath, is there for the sake of people. Law and order are not the foundation of justice, but justice is the foundation of the law. Order is not the guardian of humanness, but humanness is the guarantee of order. Any order which is devoid of justice opens the door to tyranny and becomes the instigator of the chaos and disorder it pretends to prevent.

The constitution makes the glib identification of Christianity with capitalism. Is capitalism with its overriding concern for profits and only profits, Christian? Is not God's economy an economy where people matter more than money and profits? Does not the Bible have explicit and disturbing things to say about wealth and about the rich? Over against the self-seeking, self-centered, selfish grab-ethic of capitalism, does not the gospel call us to share what we have, not to make us feel good, but in order to create equality among people (2 Cor. 8:15)? Does not the biblical ethic demand love for our neighbor, so that we first seek the interest of the neighbor instead of our own (Phil. 2:4)? Over against the capitalist theory that the rich must get richer, so that the riches may "trickle down" to the poor, stand the flaming words of the prophet Amos who did not believe that justice should "trickle down" but rather that "justice [should] roll down like waters, and righteousness like an ever-flowing stream."

Finally the constitution talks about the duty of the government and the people of South Africa to seek world peace. This is a lofty ideal, and I wish that it were true. But to begin with, we will have to state that one cannot seek peace in the world when one is the destroyer of peace at home. It seems that it is forever necessary to repeat the well-known biblical truth: peace is not simply the absence of war, it is the active presence of justice. Peace is the shalom of God for the world and for the people of his heart. It is the essence of the well-being of the community, and as such it encompasses *all* areas of life. Shalom is there also as a socio-political reality; as the gift of God which transcends any human ideas of success, it is a reality that goes beyond the purely personal and includes the totality of our human existence.

Moreover, in the Bible peace is always closely associated with *se-daqah*—justice, with which it shall join hands, according to Psalm 85:10; according to Isaiah 32:17 peace is the child of justice. So in the

Bible, peace has to do with human fulfillment, with liberation, with a meaningful life and well-being, and with the active presence of justice.

Again our question is: how can you create peace in the world when you create peace-lessness at home? The injustice of apartheid is an undeniable negation of the peace that the government is trying to seek. Apartheid, with its wanton violence, its destruction of human-being-ness, its obscene overturning of human values, is the exact opposite of peace. South Africa's policies are a threat to world peace, and certainly to the peace in this region, rather than a contribution to peace.

The essence of apartheid is the separation of people in society as well as in the church. The essence of the gospel is the truth that comes to us out of the mouth of Paul: "Jesus Christ is our peace, he who has made the two one, and has broken down the wall of enmity that has separated them."

In our situation the church must not succumb to the temptation of the false prophets who shout "Peace! Peace!" where there is no peace. As long as the false god of racial superiority rules this nation; as long as the lives of black people count for nothing and our children have to grow up with hopelessness and despair; as long as justice continues to stumble openly on the streets of this tragic, beautiful land; as long as black and white people cannot learn to live together as brothers and sisters, there shall be no peace.

Over against the deliberate lie that apartheid can create peace must stand the sober warning of Jesus Christ, once spoken to Jerusalem and sadly true of South Africa: "If you only knew the things that make for peace!"

I know about the many questions of many of us. I know about the burning uncertainties, about the understandable desire to at least know where we are going. And we long for some certainty as we face the future. But you see, the way of liberation is never a way of certainties. There is not really a blueprint. It was not true when God liberated Israel from bondage in Egypt, it is not true today. In truth, the only certainty Israel had in those days was its experience in Egypt. This is vividly recounted in the fourteenth chapter of Exodus. There Israel is caught between the advancing armies of Egypt and the sea—between the devil and the deep blue sea.

The people of Israel become desperately afraid, and in their fear long for the certainties of their life in Egypt. For there is a deadly kind of certainty in enslavement. We know the oppressor so well that we become used to a rhythm. In the process of liberation, however, there seem to be only risk and uncertainty. Besides, the power of the Pharaoh was much more concrete and tangible than the promise of God—which was all that they had, really. A promise they had not heard (only Moses had heard it), a bush they had not seen as it burned (only Moses had seen it), a land of promise which not even Moses had seen, a wilderness to go through that they did not know, and a leader whose stuttering explanations they did not trust. What was much more tangible were the fleshpots of Egypt (surely a wild exaggeration in the moment of dire distress), and the power of Egypt as represented in the king and his armies. So they shouted their anger at Moses and his God.

And poor Moses? He tries to comfort the people by promising them God's help: "The Lord will fight for you, and you must be still." But to Moses' surprise (and our own) Yahweh gets a little impatient with this comforting, pious theology. "What is the meaning of all this clamor?" Yahweh asks. "Tell the children of Israel to march." To where? Into the sea of course, and beyond the sea into the wilderness. How? Simply with faith in the promises of this God who has taken hold of this people, who has tied their future to his own, and who shall liberate those to whom he has given his heart.

No, there is still no blueprint, there is still no military strategy, there is still no certainty—there is only the promise. *And it is the people of Israel who must take up the responsibility themselves and who must march.* In faith, in trust, and in the knowledge that he is with them, determined to glorify his own name over against the might and pride of the Pharaoh.

I remind you of this story because it is so appropriate for us as we face the choices ahead of us. Behind us are the armies of the Pharaoh. In front of us the sea and the wilderness: that dark and uncertain future of which we know nothing. And the questions multiply. What if a black government is as bad as this white government? How do we know things will be different? If only we had some certainty.

But the choice is clear: we are called either to go with this God, on foot, into the sea and the wilderness, trusting only in his promises and willing to do what is right and just, or we climb onto the chariots of Pharaoh. And as with Israel, God will not make the decision for us, nor can we hope to hide behind the pious theological statements we make so often. The choice is ours, and we must not allow fear of the uncertain future to prevent us from doing what is right.

The future does not fall unexpectedly upon us, nor does it roll in on the wheels of inevitability, but it is shaped by the quality of our efforts in the present. So what South Africa will be very much depends on the kind of foundations we are today laying for that future society.

But this is a false dilemma. The question is not so much what shall we do *one day* if a black government should do something wrong. The question is what are we doing *right now,* while this white government is doing what it is doing. While it is not wrong to have a legitimate concern for the future, it *is* wrong to use that as an excuse for not being concerned about the plight of those who are the victims of oppression and exploitation right now. And it is a tortuous logic to use fear of the results of oppression as a reason for the continuation of it.

But today we have to deal with another and even more dangerous false dilemma, and that is the argument that refusal to cooperate with the government in the new constitutional plan is participation in bloody revolution.

This may be a clever political tactic, but it is as empty as it is misleading.

There is general consensus (even from "colored" supporters of the plan) that the plans are an entrenchment of white political dominance and of apartheid. What does that mean? Apartheid is an exceptionally violent political system. There is, first, the *structural* violence embedded in the laws and the structures of our society. Every law that sanctions discrimination is an act of violence. When human rights are disregarded, when education is not equal, when there is economic exploitation, when a system by design causes deprivation, malnutrition, and hunger, when the law requires the breaking up of family life—this is violence. In fact any act which erodes human dignity is an act of violence.

But second, there is also the violence needed to maintain the system, to safeguard the privileged position of the dominant group—the police and military violence without which apartheid will not survive for a single minute. We have seen it: at Sharpeville, in Soweto, in Cape Town, and we are seeing it in the ongoing civil war on the borders of Namibia.

Saying "yes" to cooperation with the very government that maintains this violent system without first fundamentally changing it is taking responsibility for the continuation of the violence. The choice for violence, therefore, has not been made by those who resist the perpetuation of the system in the hope of working for a better society, but precisely by those who have abandoned the struggle for a better society by strengthening the present one.

So let us stand firm. Let us continue to speak out for what is right. Let us continue to seek ways toward genuine peace for the people of this country, and let us continue to seek ways to break the evil cycle of violence in which we find ourselves. Let us continue to resist apartheid, to say with Gandhi that noncooperation with evil is as much a moral obligation as is cooperation with good. And let us continue to strive, to build, even now in the midst of the struggle, the foundations for genuine reconciliation between black and white in South Africa.

As you continue your work against so many odds, do not get weary. As you work in seemingly hopeless situations; as you see the light die in the eyes of those who have watched the pain too long; as you sometimes wonder whether anything at all will ever change the structures of power that so ruthlessly control our destiny in this land, do not lose faith.

Do not forget that every protest against injustice, every prayer for liberation, every act of compassion and love is an affirmation of freedom and a living sign of the kingdom of God.

And if it sometimes seems futile and the dark clouds of despair threaten to blot out the sun and your hope, remember that we are guided, not by worldly strength and power, but by faith in God who through his Son loves us and through his Spirit nurtures us, and who has given us a vision that should not die: a vision of hope, truth, love, justice, and peace. God bless you!

4

Jesus Christ, the Life of the World

Jesus Christ, the life of the world! These are words that speak of joy, of meaning, of hope. For some, they may even speak of triumph and victory. These are words that have a ring of certainty in them. Yet, in the uncertain world of suffering, oppression, and death, what do they mean? The realities of the world in which we live suggest the cold grip of death rather than the vibrant freedom of life.

Violence, greed, and the demonic distortion of human values continue to destroy God's world and his people. Economic exploitation is escalating rather than abating, and economic injustice is still the dominant reality in the relationships between rich and poor countries. Racism is as rampant as ever, not only in South Africa, but also in other parts of the world. In its alliances with national security ideologies, racism has acquired a new cloak of respectability and has become even more pervasive. In South Africa apartheid and injustice still reign supreme. Inequality is still sanctified by law, and racial superiority is still justified by theology. Today, with the blatant support of many Western governments, apartheid seems stronger than ever, and the dream of justice and human dignity for South Africa's black people seems more remote than ever.

In our world it is not the joyful, hopeful sound of the word of life that is being heard. No, that word is drowned by the ugly sound of gunfire, by the screams of our children, and by the endless cry of the powerless: "How long, Lord?"

In too many places too many children die of hunger, and too many persons just disappear because they dare to stand up for justice and human rights. Too many are swept away by the tides of war, and too many are tortured in dungeons of death. In too many eyes the years of endless struggle have extinguished the fires of hope and joy, and too

This was the riveting keynote address delivered in July 1983 at the sixth assembly of the World Council of Churches in Vancouver.

many bodies are bowed down by the weight of that peculiarly repugnant death called despair. Too many young persons believe that their youth and their future are already powdered to dust by the threat of nuclear destruction. And even in the face of all this, too many in the Christian church remain silent. We have not yet understood that every act of inhumanity, every unjust law, every untimely death, every utterance of confidence in weapons of mass destruction, every justification of violence and oppression, is a sacrifice on the altar of the false gods of death; it is a denial of the Lord of life.

No, for millions of people it is true: we are not uplifted by the word of life, we are crushed by the litany of death.

Yet the gospel affirms: Jesus Christ is the life of the world (John 6:35, 48; 10:10; 11:25; 14:6; Rev. 1:17, 18, etc.). This means he is the source of life; he is the giver of the sacred gift of life. He intends for us a life filled with abundance, joy, and meaning. He is the Messiah in whose eyes our lives are precious.

But this is precisely the problem. Dare we believe this? Can we believe this without making of our faith a narrow, spiritual escapism? Can we avoid the cynicism of "reality"? Can we find a way to live with that painful dilemma: "Lord, I believe; please help my unbelief"? And even more painful: can we accept the reality of hope and the call to battle that lie in this affirmation? In other words, is the joyous affirmation, this confession that Jesus Christ is the life of the world, really meant for the millions who suffer and die, who are oppressed and who live without hope in the world today? While discussing this theme with a group in my congregation, a woman said quietly, almost despairingly: "It seems you have to be white and rich to believe this."

Good News for the Weak

But there are two things we must remember when talking about this. First, in the Gospels this affirmation is never a triumphalistic war-cry. It is never a slogan built on might and power. It is a confession in the midst of weakness, suffering, and death. It is the quiet, subversive piety that the Christian church cannot do without. Second, we must be reminded that in the Bible this affirmation is given to people who in their situation *were* the poor, the oppressed, and the weak. They were the people who lived on the underside of history. And it is *they* who are called upon to confirm this truth: Jesus Christ is the life of the world.

In the Gospel of John, chapter 4, the story of Jesus and the Samaritan woman is a good illustration of this truth. She is the paradigm par excellence of the despised, the weak, and the oppressed, just as children are elsewhere in the Gospels. She becomes the very example of the dejected of this world. First of all, she is a woman, with all that that means in the society of her day. Notice how John makes a point of stating the disciples' astonishment that Jesus was in discussion with a woman. She is also a Samaritan, and therefore despised and rejected by the Jews. Her religion is considered inferior, and in her own community she is an outcast because of her way of life. This is probably the reason why she goes to that well alone, at a most unusual hour of the day. But it is precisely to her that Jesus speaks of these unfathomable things: the life-giving waters, and the waters of life.

Likewise, the Revelation of John is written to a weak, scattered underground church, suffering severely under the persecution of a ruthless tyrant. The followers of Jesus had no recourse, no protection under the law, no "connections" in high and powerful places, no political or economic power. Their lives were cheap. They were completely and utterly surrendered to the mercy of a man who did not know the meaning of the word, whom John could describe only with the telling title: "beast." From a purely human point of view, they had not a chance in the world. There was precious little upon which they could build their hopes for the future. But like the Samaritan woman, *they* are the ones who hear the message and to whom this is proclaimed: "I am the first and the last and the living One." They knew with a certainty not born of earthly power: Jesus Christ, not the Caesar (in spite of all *his* power!), is the life of the world. The imperial claims of divinity, of immortality, of omniscience and power are the lies, the half-truths, the propaganda without which no tyrant can survive. But the truth stands: Jesus Christ is the life of the world, and he is indeed the Lord of life.

The church understood this confession not only as comfort in times of trial and darkness but also as an essential part of that basic confession: Jesus Christ is Lord. In this way it became not only comfort to the persecuted, oppressed church but also a ringing protest against the arrogance of earthly potentates who wanted desperately to create the impression that *they* decided over the life and death of the people of God. And the church knew this confession to be the truth, not only for the life hereafter, but the truth for the very life and the very world in which they struggled to believe, to be faithful, to be obedient. To understand that is to understand the power—nay more, to experience the power—of the life-giving Word. It is to drink of the life-giving and living waters even when one is faced with suffering, destruction, and death. It is to understand and experience what it means to worship the living One in Spirit and in truth.

This worship is not confined to certain moments only. This is a worship that encompasses all of our life, so that every prayer for liberation, every act for the sake of human dignity, every commitment in the struggle for true human freedom, every protest against the sinful realities of this world becomes an offering to the living One for the sake of the kingdom.

Jesus says: "The hour comes, and it is now." Here the present and the future coincide. The moment of the hesitant yet faithful response and the moment of the favor of the Lord come together.

This is the source of the acts of sublime courage which sometimes are displayed in the witness and the life of the Christian church. This is what led to the witness of the Christian church at the martyrdom of St. Polycarp:

The blessed Polycarp died a martyr's death on the 23rd of February, on the Great Sabbath, the eighth hour. Herod imprisoned him when Phillip of Tralles was the High Priest, and Statius Quartus was the Proconsul, whilst for ever is King our Lord Jesus Christ. His be the glory, honor, majesty, and an everlasting throne from generation to generation. Amen.

And indeed it may seem as if for the moment the dictators of this world, the powerful and the mighty, have full control over this world. Their arrogance seems to have no bounds. Their power seems unchecked. But the church knows: Jesus Christ is Lord of history, he is Lord of life, and his truth shall have the final word.

In the same way Christians in South Africa are beginning to understand that for us God's moment is brought together with our present reality as we discern that the church is called to an extraordinarily courageous witness for the sake of the gospel. So we hear Bishop Desmond Tutu, the General Secretary of the South African Council of Churches, saying to the minister of law and order: "Mr. Minister, we must remind you that you are not God. You are just a man. And one day your name shall merely be a faint scribble on the pages of history, while the name of Jesus Christ, the Lord of the church, shall live forever."

The Christian church can take this stand, not because it possesses earthly power, nor because it has "control" over the situation. Over against the political, economic, and military powers that seek to rule this world, the church remains weak and in a sense defenseless. But it takes this stand because it refuses to believe that the powers of oppression, death, and destruction have the last word. Even while facing these powers the church continues to believe that Jesus Christ is Lord and therefore the life of the world. And it is this faith in the living One, this refusal to bow down to the false gods of death, that is the strength of the church.

This affirmation has another ramification. Jesus Christ is the life of the *world*. His concern is not only for the church but also for the world. In his life, death, and resurrection lies not only the future of the church, but the future of the world. In the letter to the Ephesians, Paul is persistent in proclaiming Jesus Christ as Lord of the church and of the cosmos. His being our peace has consequences not only for the church but also for the world. Therefore the church must proclaim, clearly and unequivocally, that Jesus Christ came to give meaningful life to the world, so that all human history, all human activity, can be renewed and liberated from death and destruction.

The life of the world, the destruction of this world, and the future of this world, are therefore the concern of the church. We have a responsibility for this world, for it is God's world. And if this world is threatened by the evils of militarism, materialism, greed, racism, it is very much the concern of the church. It is the church that has heard these words: "Today I am giving you a choice between good and evil, between life and death . . . choose life!" And it is the church that has heard these words: "I have come so that they may have life, and that abundantly." And because we have heard this, and because we confess Jesus Christ as the life of the world, we dare not be silent.

Speaking Out on Peace and Justice

This assembly must speak out. We must confess, humbly but without any hesitation, our faith in Jesus Christ, the life of the world. We must, humbly but without any hesitation, renew our commitment to Jesus Christ, the life of the world. And this faith, this commitment, must be the basis of our action on the issues of peace, justice, and human liberation. We must not hesitate to address ourselves to the question of peace and to the possibility of total nuclear destruction. We must be clear: the nuclear arms race, the employment of God-given human talents and possibilities for the creation of more refined weapons of mass destruction, and the call to put our faith in these weapons to secure our peace, is not simply a temporary madness; it is essentially sinful and contrary to the purposes of God for this world and for the people of his heart.

I am not persuaded that the issue of peace is simply one of fashion, a fad that will go away tomorrow. I do not agree with those who believe that this issue is simply one of political and military calculations, so that the church should withdraw from the debate and let the problems be solved by the politicians and the military strategists. I remain convinced that the issue of peace as it faces us today lies at the very heart of the gospel.

But there is something else I must say about this. When the World Alliance of Reformed Churches met in Ottawa last August, we spent considerable time discussing a statement on peace. During the debate, a delegate from Africa made a remark that very poignantly raised some of the tensions surrounding this issue in the ecumenical movement today. He said: "In this document, the word 'nuclear' is used a number of times, but I don't ever see the word 'hunger.' In my village, the people will not understand the word 'nuclear,' but they know everything about hunger and poverty."

What he was talking about was the concern of many Christians in the Third World that the issue of peace will be separated from the issue of justice, making of "peace" primarily a North Atlantic concern. This should not happen. First of all, because ideologies of militarism and national security are international in character and cause deprivation and the continuation of injustice everywhere, but especially in the so-called Third World countries. But second, and more importantly, in the Bible peace and justice are never separated. Peace is never simply the absence of war; it is the active presence of justice. It has to do with human fulfillment, with liberation, with wholeness, with a meaningful life and well-being not only for individuals, but for the community as a whole. And the prophet Isaiah speaks of peace as the offshoot of justice.

So it may be true that the issues of justice, racism, hunger, and poverty are largely unresolved issues in the ecumenical movement. It may be true that these issues present the churches with painful dilemmas, but it cannot that we will be willing to use the issue of peace to avoid those dilemmas. One cannot use the gospel to escape the demands of the gospel. And one cannot use the issue of peace to escape the unresolved issues of injustice, poverty, hunger, and racism. If we do this, we will be making of our concern for peace an ideology of oppression that in the end will be used to justify injustice.

Separating Truth from Falsehood

Jesus Christ is the life of the world because he reveals the truth about himself, the church, humankind, and the world. He is the Messiah, the chosen One of God who proclaims the acceptable year of the Lord. In him is the fulfillment of the promises of Yahweh. He is the Servant of the Lord who shall not cease his struggle until justice triumphs on the earth (Isa. 42:1-3; Matt. 12:17-21). In him shall the nations place their hope.

Jesus, in his life, death, and resurrection, is himself the guarantee of life, peace, and human dignity. He is the Messiah who struggles and suffers with his people. And yet, he is the victor. He is king in his suffering, not in spite of it. There is therefore an inseparable link between Pontius Pilate's "Ecce homo!" and his "There is your King!" (John 19:4, 19). So it is that the book of Revelation speaks of Jesus both as the lamb that was slaughtered and also as the rider on the white horse. The One who died is the One who lives forever. The suffering servant of the Lord is the ruler of the kings of the earth. The One who was willing to give up his life is Jesus the Messiah, the life of the world.

This is the truth that is revealed to the church even as we speak the words: Jesus Christ is the life of the world. The Revelation of John reminds us of the victory of the saints. But again, it is not a victory brought about by earthly powers: "They won the victory [over Satan] by the blood of the Lamb, and by the truth they proclaimed, and because they did not love their life unto death" (Rev. 12:11). This truth is the basis upon which the church stands. It is the essence of the witness of the church in the world. It is the essence of the confession: Jesus Christ is the life of the world. The church can say this only if we are willing to give our life for the sake of the world. We can say this only if we are willing to accept that the survival of the church is secondary to the survival of the world. We can say this only if we truly believe that there are some things so dear, some things so precious, some things so eternally true that they are worth dying for. And the truth that Jesus Christ is the life of the world is worth giving our life for.

The truth that the Messiah reveals is contrary to the lies, the propaganda, the idolatry, the untrustworthiness in the world. His truth is the truth that holds the freedom and the life of the world. And this we are called to proclaim. And so, as the assembled churches of the world, let us affirm this truth, and let us believe:

It is not true that this world and its inhabitants are doomed to die and be lost.
This is true: For God so loved the world that he gave his only begotten Son, that whosoever believes in him shall not perish, but have everlasting life.

It is not true that we must accept inhumanity and discrimination, hunger and poverty, death and destruction.
This is true: I have come that they may have life, and that abundantly.

It is not true that violence and hatred shall have the last word, and that war and destruction have come to stay forever.
This is true: For unto us a child is born, and unto us a Son is given, and the government shall be upon his shoulder, and his name shall be called wonderful counselor, mighty God, the everlasting Father, the Prince of peace.

It is not true that we are simply victims of the powers of evil that seek to rule the world.
This is true: To me is given all authority in heaven and on earth, and lo, I am with you always, even unto the end of the world.

It is not true that we have to wait for those who are specially gifted, who are the prophets of the church, before we can do anything.
This is true: I will pour out my Spirit on all flesh, and your sons and your daughters shall prophesy, your young men shall see visions, and your old men shall have dreams.

It is not true that our dreams for the liberation of humankind, our dreams of justice, of human dignity, of peace, are not meant for this earth and for this history.
This is true: The hour comes, and it is now, that true worshipers shall worship the Father in spirit and in truth.

So, let us dream; let us prophesy; let us see visions of love, and peace, and justice. Let us affirm with humility, with joy, with faith, with courage: *Jesus Christ, the life of the world.*

5

God Bless Africa

We have arrived at a historic moment. We have brought together under the aegis of the United Democratic Front the broadest and most significant coalition of groups and organizations struggling against apartheid, racism, and injustice since the early 1950s. We have been able to create a unity among freedom-loving people this country has not seen for many years. I am particularly happy to note that this meeting is not merely a gathering of individuals. No, we represent organizations deeply rooted in the struggle for justice, deeply rooted in the hearts of our people. Indeed, I believe we are standing at the birth of what could become the greatest and most significant people's movement in more than a quarter of a century.

We are here to say that the government's constitutional proposals are inadequate and that they do not express the will of the vast majority of South Africa's people. But more than that, we are here to say that what we are working for is one, undivided South Africa that shall belong to all of its people, an open democracy from which no single South African shall be excluded, a society in which the human dignity of all its people shall be respected. We are here to say that there are rights that are neither conferred by nor derived from the state. You have to go back beyond the dim mist of eternity to understand their origin; they are God-given. And so we are here not to beg for those rights, we are here to claim them.

In a sense, the formation of the United Democratic Front both highlights and symbolizes the crisis apartheid and its supporters have created for themselves. After a history of some 331 years of slavery, racial discrimination, dehumanization, and economic exploitation, what they expected were acceptance of the status quo, docility, and subservience. Instead they are finding a people refusing to accept racial injustice and ready to face the challenge of the moment.

The United Democratic Front was formed to bring together a wide variety of groups opposed to apartheid. This was the address Allan Boesak delivered at its inaugural meeting in Cape Town, August 20, 1983.

After more than three decades of apartheid, they expected humble submission to the harsh rule of totalitarianism and racial supremacy. Instead they find a people ready at every level of society to fight this evil system.

After more than twenty years of apartheid education they expected to see totally brainwashed, perfect little hotnotjies and kaffertjies who knew their place in the world. Instead they find a politically conscious generation of young people determined to struggle for a better future.

After the draconian measures of the 1960s and the ever harsher oppression of the so-called security laws, they expected a people immobilized by the tranquilizing drugs of apathy and fear. Instead they find a rising tide of political and human consciousness that swept away complacency and shook South Africa to its very foundations.

After the tragic happenings of the 1970s—the banning of our organizations and so many of those who struggle for justice; the torture and death of so many in detention; the merciless killing of our children on the streets of the nation—they expected surrender. Instead, here we are at this historic occasion telling South Africa and the world: we are struggling for our human dignity and for the future of our children— we shall never give up!

In all of this, those in power in this country have made the fundamental mistake of all totalitarian regimes who do not depend on the loyalty of the people but on the power of the gun: they have not reckoned with the determination of a people to be free. Because they depend on propaganda, deceit, and coercion, they have forgotten that no lie can live forever and that the fear of the gun is always overcome by the longing for freedom. They have forgotten that it is true you can kill the body, but you cannot kill the spirit and the determination of a people.

The most immediate reason for our coming together here today is the continuation of the government's apartheid policies as seen in the constitutional proposals. In recent weeks some people have asked me with greater urgency than before (and I am sure this question has been put to you also), "Why do you not see the positive side of apartheid?"

Now when you are white and your children's education is guaranteed and paid for by the state; when your job is secure and blacks are prevented from being too much competition; when your home has never been taken away and your citizenship of the country of your birth is not in danger; when your children don't have to die of hunger and malnutrition; and when your overprivileged position is guaranteed by security laws and the best equipped army on the continent, then I can understand why some people believe that apartheid has its positive side.

But for those of us who are black and who suffer under this system there is no positive side. How can we see something positive in a system which is built on oppression, injustice, and exploitation? What is positive about a system which destroys, systematically and by design, the human dignity of people, which makes as irrelevant and unimportant a thing as skin color the basis of society and the key to the understanding of human relationships, political participation, and economic justice? How can apartheid be positive when in the name of Christianity it spawns policies which cause little children to die of hunger and malnutrition, which break up black family life, and which spell out a continuous, hopeless death for millions of black people?

How can apartheid be positive when it keeps part of South Africa's children manacled in the chains of unfreedom and the other part in the chains of fear? The time has come for white people to realize that their destiny is inextricably bound with our destiny and that they shall never be free until we are free. I am so happy that so many of our white brothers and sisters are saying this by their presence here today.

It is true: people who think that their security and peace lie in the perpetuation of intimidation, dehumanization, and violence, are *not* free. They will never be free as long as they have to kill our children in order to safeguard their overprivileged positions. They will never be free as long as they have to lie awake at night worrying whether a black government will one day do the same to them as they are doing to us, when white power will have come to its inevitable end.

But we must also ask the question: what is positive about the government's constitutional proposals? In order that there should be no misunderstanding, let me as clearly and briefly as possible repeat the reasons why we reject these proposals.

—Racism, so embedded in South African society, is once again written into the constitution. All over the world, people are beginning to recognize that racism is politically untenable, sociologically unsound, and morally unacceptable. But in this country, the doctrine of racial supremacy, although condemned by most churches in South Africa as heresy and idolatry, is once again enshrined in the constitution as the basis upon which to build the further development of our society and the nurturing of human relationships.

—All the basic laws, those laws which are the very pillars of apartheid, indeed, those laws without which the system cannot survive—mixed marriages, group areas, racial classification, separate and unequal education, to name but a few—remain untouched and unchanged.

—The homelands policy, which is surely the most immoral and objectionable aspect of the apartheid policies of the government, forms the basis for the willful exclusion of 80 percent of our nation from the new political deal. Indeed, in the words of the proposals made by the president's council, the homelands policy is to be regarded as "irreversible." So our African brothers and sisters will be driven even further into the wilderness of homeland politics; millions will have to find their political rights in the sham independence of those bush republics; millions more will continue to lose their South African citizenship; and millions more will be forcibly removed from their homes into resettlement camps.

—Clearly the oppression will continue, the brutal breakup of black family life will not end. The apartheid line is not at all abolished; it is simply shifted so as to include those so-called coloreds and Indians who are willing to cooperate with the government.

—Not only is the present system of apartheid given more elasticity, making fundamental change even harder than before, but in the new proposals the dream of democracy to which we strive is still further eroded.

—So while the proposals may mean something for those middle-class blacks who think that the improvement of their own economic position is the highest good, it will not bring any significant changes to the life of those who have no rights at all, who must languish in the poverty and utter destitution of the homelands, and who are forbidden by law to live together as families in what is called "white South Africa."

It cannot be repeated often enough that all South Africans who love this country and who care for its future, black and white, Jew and Gentile, Christian and Muslim, have no option but to reject these proposals.

Apartheid is a cancer in the body politic of the world, a scourge on our society, and an everlasting shame to the church of Jesus Christ in the world and in this country. It exists only because of economic greed, cultural chauvinism, and political oppression, maintained by both systemic and physical violence and a false sense of racial superiority. And therefore we must resist it. We must resist it because it is in fundamental opposition to the noble principles of our Judeo-Christian heritage, and of the Muslim faith. We must resist it because it is a fundamental denial of all that is worthwhile and human in our society. It is in opposition to the will of God for this country. We must resist it because in its claim to be Christian apartheid is a blasphemy, idolatry, and a heresy.

To be sure, the new proposals will make apartheid less blatant in some ways. It will be modernized and streamlined, and in its new multicolored cloak it will be less conspicuous and less offensive to some. Nonetheless, it will still be there. And we must remember, apartheid is a thoroughly evil system. As such it cannot be modified, modernized, or streamlined; it has to be irrevocably eradicated. And we must continue to struggle until that glorious day shall dawn when apartheid shall exist no more.

And so, to those who ask *why* we are not satisfied and *when* we shall be satisfied we must say in clear, patient terms: we shall not be satisfied as long as injustice reigns supreme on the throne of our land. We shall not be satisfied as long as those who rule us are not inspired by justice but dictated to by fear, greed, and racialism. We shall not be satisfied until South Africa is once again one, undivided country, a land where there shall be meaningful participation in a democratic process of government for all our people.

We shall not be satisfied until the wealth and riches of this country are shared by all. We shall not be satisfied until justice rolls down like waters and righteousness like a mighty stream.

We must turn to one other important question, namely the question of whites and blacks working together. This has been mentioned as a reason why the United Democratic Front has been so severely attacked by some and why they have refused to give their cooperation.

They are saying to us that white people cannot play a meaningful role in the struggle for justice in this country because they are always, by definition, the oppressor. Because the oppression of our people wears a white face, because the laws are made by a white government, because we are suffering so much under a system created and maintained by white people, they say there can be no cooperation between white and black until all of this is changed.

I would like to say to those who think this way that I understand the way they feel. We have seen with our own eyes the brutalization of our people at the hands of whites. We have seen police brutality. We have experienced the viciousness and the violence of apartheid. We have been trampled on for so long; we have been dehumanized for so long. But it is not true that apartheid has the support of all white people. There are those who have struggled with us, who have gone to jail, who have been tortured and banned. There are those who have died in the struggle for justice. And we must not allow our anger for apartheid to become the basis for a blind hatred for *all* white people. Let us not build our struggle upon hatred, bitterness, and a desire for revenge. Let us even now seek to lay the foundation for reconciliation between white and black in this country by working together, praying together, struggling together for justice.

No, the nature and the quality of our struggle for liberation cannot be determined by the color of one's skin, but rather by the quality of one's commitment to justice, peace, and human liberation. And in the final analysis, judgment will be given, not in terms of whiteness or blackness, whatever the ideological content of those words may be today, but in terms of the persistent faithfulness we are called to in this struggle.

Besides, the very fact that we are talking about the constitutional proposals already reveals the paradox in this argument. The government has been pushing ahead with these proposals precisely because they have been supported and accepted by some people from the black community who think that the short-term economic gains and the semblance of political power are more important than the total liberation of all South Africa's people. So our struggle is not only against the white government and their plans, but also against those in the black community who through their collaboration seek to give credibility to these plans.

But there is something else that we must say. South Africa belongs to all its people. That is a basic truth we must cling to tenaciously for now and for the future. This country is our country, and its future is not safe in the hands of people who—white or black—despise democracy and trample on the rights of the people. Its future is not safe in the hands of people—white or black—who depend upon economic exploitation and human degradation to build their empires. Its future is not safe in the hands of people—white or black—who need the flimsy and deceitful cloak of ethnic superiority to cover the nakedness of their racialism. Its future is not safe in the hands of people—white or black—who seek to secure their unjustly required privileged positions by violent repression of the weak, the exploited, and the needy. Its future is not safe in the hands of people—white or black—who put their faith simply in the madness of growing militarism. So for the sake of our country and our children, whether *you* be white or black, resist those people, whether *they* be white or black.

So let us not be fearful of those who sit in the seats of power, their lips dripping with the words of interposition and nullification. Let us not be intimidated by those who so arrogantly, so frighteningly, echo their master's voice.

We are doing what we are doing not because we are white or black, we are doing what we are doing *because it is right.* And we shall continue to do so until justice and peace embrace and South Africa becomes the nation it is meant to be.

In the meantime let me remind you of three little words, words that express so eloquently our seriousness in this struggle. You don't have to have a vast vocabulary to understand them. You don't need a philosophical bent to grasp them—they are just three little words. The first word is the word *ALL.* We want *all* of our rights. Not just some rights, not just a few token handouts the government sees fit to give—we want all our rights. And we want *all* of South Africa's people to have their rights. Not just a selected few, not just "coloreds" or "Indians" after they have been made honorary whites. We want the rights of all South Africa, including those whose citizenship has already been stripped away by this government.

The second word is the word *HERE.* We want all of our rights *here,* in a united, undivided South Africa. We do not want them in impoverished homelands, we don't want them in our separate little group areas. We want them here in this land which one day we shall once again call our own.

The third word is the word *NOW.* We want all of our rights, we want them here, and we want them now. We have been waiting so long, we have been struggling so long. We have pleaded, cried, petitioned too long now. We have been jailed, exiled, killed for too long. Now is the time! And as we struggle let us remember that change does not roll in on the wheels of inevitability. It comes through the tireless efforts and hard work of those who are coworkers with God, who are willing to take the risk of fighting for freedom, democracy, and human dignity.

As we struggle on let us continue to sing that wonderful hymn of freedom: Nkosi Sikilel í Afriká. I know: today we are singing that hymn with tears in our eyes. We are singing it while we are bowed down by the weight of oppression and battered by the winds of injustice. We are singing it while our old people languish in the resettlement camps and our children are dying of hunger in the homelands. We are singing it now while we suffer under the brutality of apartheid and while the blood of our children is calling to God from the streets of our nation.

But we must work for the day when we shall sing it when we are free. We shall sing it when our children shall no longer be judged by the color of their skin but by the humanness of their character.

We shall sing it on that day when we even here in this country, in Johannesburg and Cape Town, in Port Elizabeth and Durban, the sanctity of marriage and family life shall be respected, and no law shall require of man to put asunder what God has joined together.

We shall sing it on that day when in this rich land no child shall die of hunger and no infant shall die untimely, and our elderly shall close their eyes in peace, and the wrinkled stomachs of our children shall be filled with food just as their lives shall be filled with meaning.

We shall sing it when here in South Africa white and black will have learned to love one another and work together in building a truly good and beautiful land.

With this faith, we shall yet be able to give justice and peace their rightful place on the throne of our land; with this faith, we shall yet be able to see beyond the darkness of our present into the bright and glittering daylight of our future; with this faith we shall be able to speed up the day when all of South Africa's children will embrace each other and sing with new meaning:

NKOSI SIKILEL Í AFRIKÁ
GOD BLESS AFRICA—GUIDE HER RULERS—BLESS HER
CHILDREN—GIVE HER PEACE!

6

A Holy Rage for Justice

A Bookshop in Kampen

"It is better to damage Denmark's relations with Germany than to damage Denmark's relationship with Jesus Christ." These words jumped out at me as I stood in a bookshop in Kampen, the Netherlands, leafing through a little book with the title "Long Live Life." It was a book of translations of sermons and articles by a man called Kaj Munk, the father of Danish resistance to Adolf Hitler during the Nazi period.

I was fascinated by what I read. I had never heard of Kaj Munk before. I had studied in Holland, in this same Kampen, a famous old university town, for six years. In all those years I had not known about Kaj Munk, what he did, what he stood for, and how he lived and died. During my years of study, I had heard of Dietrich Bonhoeffer. I had read some of his works and I was deeply impressed by this man, his courage and his witness. I knew at once that we in South Africa, with our own struggle against the forces of violence, racialism, and totalitarianism, could learn much from him. But this was 1979. My own role in the struggle for liberation in South Africa as a Christian was just becoming more clearly defined. Just that July I had spoken before the National Conference of the South African Council of Churches calling for the church to become meaningfully involved in the struggle for liberation. I had challenged the churches to initiate campaigns for civil disobedience to seek change in South Africa. I had been severely attacked by the government press, and the minister of justice publicly warned the churches—and me in particular—to be careful. In response I had written an open letter to the minister stating my position on these issues.

In 1983, Allan Boesak was the first recipient of the Kaj Munk Award, inaugurated in honor of the Danish pastor and World War II resistance activist. In 1984, the theological faculty of the University of the Western Cape, where Boesak was student chaplain, held a Kaj Munk Week. Boesak delivered this address on March 9, 1984.

And here I was reading of a man who was as much involved in the struggle for truth and freedom as was Dietrich Bonhoeffer, and with as much to teach us in South Africa as Bonhoeffer. Here I was reading his letter to *his* minister for church affairs, written in 1943. The situation was amazingly like ours in South Africa. The instructions given by the minister were exactly the same given to me by minister Schlebusch: ministers of the gospel should keep out of politics. Kaj Munk's reply sounded with the clarity of a trumpet: "If I, out of fear for human beings, should restrict myself to the role of inactive spectator, it would be a crime inflicted upon my Christian faith, my Danish patriotism, and my solemn oath as a pastor of the church. It is better to damage Denmark's relations with Germany than to damage Denmark's relationship with Jesus Christ."

I was deeply moved by so much prophetic clarity, so much courage, so much trust in the God of Christ. Here was a man who knew where his allegiance and his obedience lay. Here was a man whose love for truth and for the God of truth had overcome his fear for the ruthless, violent tyrants who ruled Germany and Denmark at the time. Here was a man whose witness is a call upon all in South Africa who love the Lord of justice and peace, an inspiration to all who seek to do his will in our own struggle for liberation and human dignity.

I will never understand why it is that it had taken me so long to discover Kaj Munk. Nor will I understand why he, in contrast to Bonhoeffer, has been so quickly forgotten by the church ecumenical. It seems to me that Munk has a lot to say to the ecumenical movement in general and to South African Christians in particular.

A Theological Maverick

One reason why Kaj Munk does not play so prominent a role today may be the unsystematic way in which he did his theology—and the disdain with which he regarded the theology of Europe. He certainly had no respect for historical-critical methods of exegesis: "Even at our little university here in Copenhagen there are still people who, at the expense of our empty national coffers, sit there night and day messing about with St. Paul's buts and ifs, an activity which proves beyond doubt how right Paul was when he wrote that the letter kills the spirit."

Systematic theology, he felt, is the "way of the devil to further Christianity." The way New Testament scholars treated the Bible was

like a "crossword puzzle," not much different from "blasphemy." In
one of his dramas a pastor says, "I have been trained in theology, which
is to say in nonspirituality and nonsense." In a meeting with colleagues
he exclaimed: "A minister of the gospel who remains stuck in the mud
of theology will never come to mean anything much to the kingdom of
God." I can understand that such open disdain for the theology of which
Western Europe had become so proud would not endear Munk to these
theologians whose whole life was this kind of theology. Kaj Munk just
would not take them as seriously as they took themselves.

But there may have been something else. Kaj Munk had a simple,
direct, and very personal relationship with Jesus Christ, and he spoke
about it in a way that would often be embarrassing to many, especially
those whom one could call "professional theologians." His was a language that did not fit into the scientific mode in which theology is done:
"I believe in God the Father, the Creator of heaven and earth. . . . One
person taught me that and paid the full price to teach me that. . . .
When I was a child, I accepted that on the authority of my mother, but
as I grew older, I learned to know a heart that beat more warmly than
even that of my mother. . . . That was the heart of Jesus Christ." Such
is not the language that gains one entry into the hallowed ranks of what
are called "theologians."

A final reason for the relative silence about Munk today, even in
Denmark, may be his acceptance of violence as a response to violence
brought on by tyranny and oppression. I have a suspicion that Christians
in Denmark and in Europe in general may have great difficulty in making a hero of a man who preached revolution and who called his people
to rebellion against Hitler, while Danish churches today are among
those who are most preoccupied with the peace issue.

A False Dilemma

I believe this may be false dilemma. The situations now and then are
completely different. During the second world war, Denmark opted for
neutrality and made a nonaggression pact with the Germans. After the
occupation of Denmark on April 9, 1940, and the subsequent oppression in Denmark by the Germans, it became clear that pacts with the
devil are as worthless as the paper they are written on. In situations
like those, neutrality is criminal and pacifism becomes less and less an
option. In the face of an evil like Nazism, witnessing the continued

oppression, indeed the obliteration of the Jews, being drawn relentlessly into the vortex of war, how many choices does one really have? When pacts and promises are no longer honored, when truth is crucified and the lie reigns supreme upon the throne of the land, when one is not governed, but ruled by a tyrant, how many choices does one have? When the tyrant is so bent on violence, so endlessly arrogant that he cannot respond humanly to suffering, to pleas for mercy, and to the call for justice, how many choices does one have? When there is a war on, and neutrality and passivity in the name of some philosophical principle actually become collaboration with the oppressor while the innocent die: how many choices does one have?

Kaj Munk knew, and those of us who live in situations like these today know: not many. We understand Kaj Munk as he agonizes over the decision he must make:

> When fire and murder are unleashed upon the people of the earth, it is our task to denounce, in the name of the God of love, everything which we know to be the work of the devil. When the deck is loaded, when cowardice heaps praises upon that which before was recognized as despicable, then it is the task of the church to realize that the signs of the church have always been the dove, the lamb, the lion, and the fish, but never the chameleon.

Our argument is that in situations like those the choices are often made for us, when the use of violence, as difficult as this may be, is forced upon us by the oppressor. It is then, when options are so agonizingly narrowed down, that those with a sense of justice and with a vision for what should be could find themselves driven to take up arms.

This does not mean that Kaj Munk would naturally have chosen for counter violence. Today, I believe, he would have been with those of us in the peace movement, fighting for the survival of humankind, for the preservation of the earth against the madness of nuclear armament, and therefore for the preservation of our humanity. His love for nature, his fascination with and appreciation for its beauty, his love for humankind, his passion for justice, and above all, Munk's love for God and his humble willingness to listen to the Word of God for every situation in which he found himself—these are, I believe, the reasons why I do not doubt where Munk would have stood today. We should not pin him down on issues and in situations of forty years ago that can in no way be compared with our own.

Munk would not only have done this, he would also have understood

fully the situations of many Christians in the Third World who face the
same kind of evil oppression today that the Danes saw in Hitler and
Nazism. He would have understood the terrible loneliness of making
choices, the unbearable tensions between what we believe to be the
demands of the gospel, namely to choose for peace and reconciliation
which exclude the use of violence, and on the other hand the grim
realization that you are facing an oppressor who does not, cannot, and
will not respond to nonviolent pressures for change, to pleas for justice
and mercy, and to appeals from the heart of the gospel.

Should the churches in Western Europe recognize this contribution
of Kaj Munk, and should the churches in North America come to know
him, and should all these churches really begin to take Munk seriously,
I have no doubt that the ecumenical debate on the Program to Combat
Racism would take on a completely different character. It could open
the way for a new understanding of Christian solidarity within the ecumenical movement. Munk can become the bridge between Christians
from different parts of the world. But only as he is being taken seriously, as his theology becomes real for the churches of Europe, and as
the churches in Europe learn again what it means to take the risk of
divine obedience.

Divine Obedience—Disobedience

For this is one of the reasons why Munk's example is such an inspiration
to me particularly: he understood the risks of faith and he understood
the joys of faith. His struggle was for justice, for freedom, but it was
rooted in his faith in the gospel of Jesus the Messiah. Therefore he
understood that it was the joy of faith that led to the struggle for justice;
it was the love of God which led to the passion for freedom. It was
obedience to God which led to the disobedience to earthly powers who
challenge the Word of the Living One. His faith in Jesus Christ, re-
joicing in the certainty of the resurrection, knowing that Jesus Christ
is indeed the life of the world—that became the basis for his courage:

Jesus Christ is risen. For that faith I shall fight, against the world, and against
myself. . . . On this faith I build my hope, for myself and for humanity.

It was this courage that led him to write his famous letter to the
minister for church affairs in which he addressed the minister as a
prophet of God and a pastor of the church. With cool, calm clarity he

explained that he would not obey the order to keep out of politics. Instead he would honor the head of the Lutheran Church in Norway, whose arrest (for what the Germans called "political activity") was the direct cause for the circular letter which contained the order. Kaj Munk wrote:

> I have the honor to inform you that I am not only of the opinion that I should not obey [that order] but that I shall act expressly against it. For we as ministers of the gospel are called to preach the Word [of God] and not to silence it. To accept injustice shall have the most dire consequences for our country and for our people.

Munk could have written this to the South African government. At a time when the churches in South Africa are becoming more involved than ever in the struggle for liberation and justice, and when the black church has become such an important vehicle for the expression of the political and human aspirations of millions of black people in South Africa, the tensions between the church and the government are fast reaching boiling point.

Many is the time that the government has warned clergy to "stay out of politics"; clergy and other church workers have been detained and tortured, some have been banned, others have been harassed in different ways. The government has instituted a commission of inquiry into the work of the South African Council of Churches, and it is almost certain that the commission will come to the government with harsh recommendations to curtail the work of the council and to scare the churches into submission and silence. Bishop Desmond Tutu has correctly observed that it is "our Christian faith that is on trial here." For the churches are involved in the political scene in South Africa, not because we want to "play politics," but because the politics of the South African government are unjust and inhuman, they cause discrimination, deprivation, and exploitation on a large scale, and they are the cause of the violence which is so endemic to South Africa's apartheid society.

Furthermore, the South African government claims to be a "Christian" government; the people who vote for it call themselves Christians; the abhorrent policies of this government are executed in the name of Jesus Christ. This lie needs to be exposed over and over again. Apartheid needs to be called by its real name: a cancer in the body politic of the world, a shame to the Christian church in South Africa and in its claim to be Christian, an idolatry, a heresy, and a blasphemy. It is as evil as Nazism. There may be people who find it expedient to ignore the evils of this system or to be silent out of fear of the ruthlessness of the government. The church in South Africa has no choice but to say with Kaj Munk:

> We stand in the temple of the eternal God. All others have their obligations to this and to that; we alone have our obligations exclusively to the truth.

The truth Kaj Munk speaks about is, I think, the truth that Jesus Christ alone is Lord. He is the Lord of life, and he is the life of the world. This is our joy, this is our strength. It is the truth that makes us believe in him as the liberator God. It is the truth that says to us that God is not honored by illness, by poverty, dejection, and exploitation. God is not honored by death and destruction, by the inhumanity of apartheid. God is not honored by the untimely death of little children who suffer hunger while the tables of the rich are sagging under the weight of surplus food. God is not honored by the naked cynicism of those who seek peace through the terror of the nuclear threat.

No, these are the lies we are called to unmask. We are obliged to tell the truth, to shout it from the rooftops. The truth is that God is honored when we create peace on earth for *all* people in whom he has placed his favor. He is honored when the hungry are fed, when the poor and oppressed may taste the sweet fruits of justice. He is honored when the prisoners are set free, when the exiled may return home in peace and safety. He is honored when sinners repent and find forgiveness and reconciliation, when the broken-hearted are healed and become whole again, when the lonely and dejected discover communion and closeness with others and in so doing discover their own human-beingness. God is honored when we, the people of this world, discover the joy of being the people of his favor. It is this truth which Jesus the Messiah has disclosed to his church, and it is this truth which the church is called to proclaim and to which we are exclusively obligated. And in so proclaiming we discover the One who said, "I am the way, the truth, the life." Knowing this is knowing obedience. Knowing this obedience is understanding the call to disobey all who would want to kill or defy this truth.

Where Is God?

But let no one think that Munk had a triumphalistic Jesus-is-the-answer theology. Of course, in the end he discovered, like we all do, that Jesus *is* indeed the answer. But not in the simplistic, glib way which has made of this truth the superficial slogan it has become. It is something one discovers only in the depth of pain, in the agony of uncertainty, in the search for hope amid the hopelessness to which faith can bring us. It is despair which arrives as we discover that we don't understand God or what he is doing in the world, the despair in which we find that to appeal against God we have to appeal to God.

We see him fleeing his church in Vedersö so that they could call a more believing, better pastor—one who did not feel doubt about himself, his own abilities, and his faith gnawing at his guts day and night. Yet he could not stay away, nor could he escape his calling. The prophet, he wrote, knows that he has been sent by the One who calls himself "I AM WHO I AM"—the One who has overcome him, the One who does not brook resistance. He calls, I must obey.

His faith grew out of that constant battle between him and the God who refused to let go of him. Munk knew him to be the God of Jesus Christ, and yet he knew moments when the tormenting question was uppermost in his mind: where is God? Looking at the world, wrestling with the presence of so much injustice, pain, and suffering, he went to court with God, to God.

> The poison gas of the Japanese destroys the Chinese; in Spain little children die miserably; for the last eighteen years the wife of the blacksmith is suffering from an incurable disease; the young couple who were so radiant on their wedding day are now making hell for themselves out of their marriage; young girls play with fire and bury their children while still alive in the dung-heap; and in my own heart, purified as it is by the water of baptism, lurks lust, revenge, arrogance, and self-destruction. No, we do not understand him. We don't understand why he is silent, why he has not long ago strangled the devil.

These are bitter questions indeed, put as plainly as in the Psalms, to a God who is the same God with whom the prophets wrestled, at whom they shouted, to whom they prayed, in whose response and love they found an answer. Like Jeremiah, who found the answer to his own pain in the truth that "thou hast made me thine" (Jer. 15:16), Munk discovers the answer in the love of God:

> The church stands in the midst of this same world of self-preservation, struggle, and sin, showing the way that leads to God. And even if his garment radiates the coldness of eternity [i.e., the suffering and pain in the world] for those who hide there, they will discover that it is precisely there [in the midst of the suffering] that one feels the beat of the warm, living heart. And this warmth is the warmth of Golgotha's blood.

For Munk it was no esoterical, pie-in-the-sky theology which served as an opiate for a suffering, oppressed people. This answer did not drive him out of the world into an empty religiosity where he became estranged from the world and the problems of the world. On the contrary, this faith led to a new understanding: that God was present in the midst of pain, terror, suffering, and threat of death, not to sanction and placate, but to overturn and comfort. It was not a legitimizing presence, but a protesting presence. It was not to say "Be still," but it was to say "Don't accept it!"

When Kaj Munk posed the question "Where is God?" and found the answer in the love of Jesus on the cross of Golgotha, it led him inexorably, inevitably to that day in October 1943 when he spoke the words which changed his life and the direction of his struggle against Hitler:

When here in our country compatriots are being persecuted simply on the basis of their racial origin, then it is the Christian duty of the church to call out: this is in opposition to the laws of love and mercy, it is abhorrent to our free, Danish spirit. And the church may and must go further without permitting anyone to stop her: if this continues, we shall, with God's help, move the people to rebellion.

This was the ultimate consequence of his obedience to God that Kaj Munk was called to in this particular situation.

Toward the end of November I was in a place called Mogopa in the Western Transvaal. We went to pray with the people of that settlement because they were going to be forcibly removed from their homes by the South African government. As I stood there, watching the helplessness of those people who were so vulnerable, so defenseless against this powerful, ruthless government, I asked myself the question, "Where is the God of justice, mercy, and love?" As I saw the people breaking down their own homes I was overcome with a nameless and deep despair. Isn't there anything else we could do except pray with these people, assuring them that God is just, that he is love, that he is on their side? As we have been doing all night long? This was also the question put to me by a journalist.

Then I thought about Kaj Munk, and I knew and told him: sometimes there is nothing else the church can do. Sometimes there is nothing else that the church *must* do than to pray with the people, to assure them that God is not aloof but present in their situation, in their pain, that he is sharing their pain and despair, that he is with them—not to bless the lie that was happening to them, but to remind them that the truth that is being crushed to earth shall rise again. But this is subversive piety, which always leads to the resistance of evil, not because of hatred, but because of the protesting presence of the loving God.

It is the same subversive piety we discover in the Heidelberg Catechism when it asks the question: "What is my only comfort in life and death?" The answer is: "That I, with body and soul, in life and in death, am not my own, but belong to my faithful Savior Jesus Christ; who with his blood has fully atoned for all my sins, and delivered me from the power of the devil, and so preserves me that without the will of my heavenly Father not a hair can fall from my head; yea, that all things must be subservient to my salvation, wherefore by his Holy Spirit he also assures me of eternal life, and makes me heartily willing and ready, henceforth, to live unto him."

A Holy Rage

In South Africa the words of Kaj Munk, spoken more than forty years ago, remain wondrously, dangerously relevant. The church is called to seek justice, to seek liberation for the oppressed, to seek reconciliation as her Lord had done.

We are called to participate in the struggle for justice and human dignity. In all of this the minister of the gospel has a special responsibility. Like Kaj Munk, we live in times when the old answers to important and vexing questions can no longer suffice. Like Kaj Munk, we are forced to ask anew: what is the task of the minister of the gospel in South Africa today? How shall we face the changing situation? What do we say when, as in Nazi-occupied Denmark, "the lie rages across the face of the earth?" How do we preach when some of our own people, for the sake of material gain and the taste of political power, will sell all that is dear and precious for a mess of apartheid potage, by joining the government in its new constitutional system? What do we say when it becomes clearer and clearer that the government is bent on using the church and our message as part of the propaganda to further the lie of the "total onslaught"? When, paradoxically but perfectly understandably, we in the church who resist apartheid become part of the "total onslaught" ourselves? Again, what is the task and the responsibility of the preacher in South Africa today?

I cannot but answer with the words of Kaj Munk: "For what we as pastors lack is not psychology or literature. We lack a holy rage."

A holy rage. That anger which comes from God—from the knowledge of God and humanity, says Munk. The ability to rage when justice lies prostrate on the streets of our nation. To rage when families are broken up through influx control laws and mothers with little babies are tear-gassed, threatened with dogs and guns, arrested at three in the morning, and separated from their children as they are being carted off to jail, simply because they are black. To rage when in this rich land children must die of hunger. To rage when old people must be removed by force from ancestral lands, to languish a slow death in the desolation of a concentration camp called, euphemistically, a "resettlement area." To rage when millions lose, at the stroke of a willful ministerial pen, their citizenship of the land of their birth. To rage against the inhumanity and violence of apartheid. To cry for the loss of love and future. To rage against the misuse of God's holy gospel which is the Word of life. To rage against the complacency of a church that fails to realize that our country shall live only by the truth, and that our fear shall be the death of us all.

What is therefore the task of the preacher today? Shall I answer: faith, hope, and love? That sounds beautiful. But I would rather say: courage. No, even that is not challenging enough to be the *whole* truth. My dear colleagues, our task today is: recklessness.

And that's the truth. Oh, for Kaj Munk to live again—in South Africa.

7

Between Faith and Despair

When Jesus had finished giving his twelve disciples their instructions, he left that place and went to teach and preach in the neighboring towns.

John, who was in prison, heard what Christ was doing, and sent his own disciples to him with a message: "Are you the one who is to come, or are we to expect some other?" Jesus answered, "Go and tell John what you hear and see: the blind recover their sight, the lame walk, the lepers are made clean, the deaf hear, the dead are raised to life, the poor are hearing the good news—and happy is the man who does not find me a stumbling-block."

Matthew 11:1-6

I have talked before about the dream of God for his world. It is a dream which spells out as clearly as possible the actions of God in the world and how God overturns human history and overturns human life to become involved with him in his actions in the world. I have talked about the way the dream is threatened because the world is threatened by the dream. But that threat comes from the outside, as it were—evil forces outside who cannot respond to the dream and therefore have to kill the dreamer.

But here I want to deal with something from within that can be just as threatening to the dream and to the reality the dream represents in the world. Doubt and uncertainty have always been part of the lives of those who believe. Many times we suddenly find ourselves asking the question: is it really worthwhile? Is there something that I can believe in which makes sense? Does my faith make sense in the world?

All of us have had times when we saw too many things happening in the world which we could not explain, too many things which were quite in contradiction to our faith in a God who loves, who cares, and who has compassion for his world.

Prior to the July 1984 gathering of the Lutheran World Federation in Budapest, there was a pre-assembly gathering of young people at which Allan Boesak participated in a series of Bible studies. This was his second address to the young people on that occasion.

Life-and-Death Struggle with Faith

I am not talking about those intellectual discussions which I know that some of you have from time to time, when you sit back with a bottle of beer or when you really "la-dee-da" with a glass of sherry and talk about the irrelevancy of faith these days. I am not talking about that kind of intellectual exercise.

I am talking about the life-and-death struggle with faith and with God, because we know that even though there are things that we do not understand, we have to struggle with God because there is nothing else for us to do. Faith in God is the only thing we have that makes sense. But here is the problem if you believe in God: it is God that you have to fight with. This happens over and over again in the Bible. I do not think that when those moments come we should deny them.

It is amusing how theologians try to cover up for John. They try to tell us that he was not really in doubt. No, they say, it was really his disciples who did not understand what was happening. So John, in order to help his disciples, sent them to Jesus with the question we find in verse two: "Are you the one who is to come, or are we to expect some other?" Therefore the doubt of John was not really doubt, they say; it was simply pastoral concern for his disciples that made him ask that question. He was only trying to get them to discover the truth.

I do not belive that.

Jesus says to John's disciples: go and tell John what you hear and see! Jesus knew the source of the doubt was not so much the disciples, although they may also have doubted the point. The real doubter was John. And it is common that people in the Bible find themselves in a situation like that.

Elijah, after that exhilarating experience on the top of Mount Carmel, finds himself under a broom tree saying to God: "I wish I could die because all of this is not worth it! Jezebel is going to get me ashore as the sun comes up in the morning."

Jeremiah, my favorite prophet, finds himself in a similar situation. He is suddenly confronted with realities in his life that he had not counted on. He did not bargain for the experiences that he had to go through, and he knows that he cannot struggle with people about that. He has to talk with God, and he says to God, "You have deceived me," as our translation reads. But that is not the word Jeremiah uses. He says, "You have seduced me! And I have allowed myself to be seduced."

This is a heavy word. And he goes on to say to God: "You have become to me like a deceitful brook, waters that I cannot depend upon. When I want to drink of this water, it disappears, it dries up." In his struggle with God he has to find a way out of his doubt and uncertainty. He knows the only way to do it is to grapple with his God, to get hold of God and pull and not to let go until that moment finds an answer that makes sense.

We find this same doubt also in the Psalms. I say we must learn to deal with it. Christians have a tendency to run away from such feelings, because we believe we ought not to feel this way. We must always be very faithful; we must always believe everything—and if we doubt for one minute, God will somehow get us.

The Need for Anger

We must not be like that. It is as if we do not know how to deal with anger. We do not want to become angry—Christians do not get angry; Christians do not get upset. We may feel a little disturbed sometimes, but we never get angry. And we have to smile all the time. I like to smile, but there are times when we must not run away from legitimate feelings of doubt, uncertainty, and anger.

Kaj Munk is a man that I have discovered only late in my life, and I am sorry about that. Kaj Munk was a pastor in the Danish church who just before and during the war became a spiritual inspiration to the resistance of the Danish people to Nazi Germany. Eventually, in January 1944, he was taken away by the Gestapo and shot in the fields of Jutland. But Kaj Munk said to his colleagues in the church: "What we need in the church—and I am saying the same to you—is not more literature and psychology. What we need is a holy rage." Kaj Munk is right!

We need to get angry about the things that are wrong in this world. We need to rage about the way the innocent continue to die. We need to rage about the injustices that seem to multiply every day. We need to get angry at the fact that the powerful and the mighty seem to be able to get away with anything, including murder. We need to get angry about the fact that because people have power and might, they think they can trample on the lives of God's people who are defenseless. We need to get angry about systems in the world that continue poverty and deprivation for millions of God's children.

One of the problems I have with the Christian church is that we do not get angry enough. There is not enough rage in us. We must remember that twice in the Bible we read these words, first in Jeremiah and then in the Gospel of Matthew: Rachel mourns over her children and refuses to be comforted. Something of that we must learn to have in our lives. We must learn what it means to mourn, or to rage, or to refuse to be comforted by the cheap words that we so often use.

When something happens, the first thing Christians do is to grab ourselves a Bible text and to dish it out to people like cheap medicine in a state-subsidized clinic. We must not do that! We must struggle with the pain, with the anger, and with the doubt that comes with it. I believe that it is out of this struggle with God that the protest against the misery, the suffering, and the senseless pain in the world is born.

We must understand John. He answered God's call to preach the gospel to the world. He was the one who was called by God to testify to the life that had come. He was the messenger that the prophet Micah spoke about, who would go ahead of the Messiah. He saw clearly before anyone else and said it out loud: "Here is the lamb of God who shall take away the sins of the world!"

He was the one who had enough guts to preach this gospel without any compromise. He had the courage to tell Pharisees: "Do not think that because you are children of Abraham, God will accept you just like that! God has the power to make out of these stones children of Abraham. There is nothing inherently in you that must cause God to be with you on your side. You need to have a conversion. You need to change your life. You need to become again like the very people you despise, namely the poor, the dejected, and the despised."

He spoke not only to the Pharisees, but he spoke also to King Herod. He did not simply admonish King Herod because the man lived with his brother's wife. The Gospel says clearly that he struggled with this King, that he attacked and admonished him because of all the wrong that Herod was doing. It was because of this that John found himself in prison. I can understand that while he was in prison, knowing that his very life was at stake there and perhaps knowing that he would never leave the prison alive, he sat there thinking: "Must my life come to this? Is this what I have worked for? Is this how the kingdom of God is realized in the world? What does it help now that the Messiah is in the world and I have given all that I have—and still I must die in this fashion?"

A Nameless Sense of Despair

I can understand why he asked Jesus: "Are you the one who is to come or are we to expect some other?" If the Messiah is really in the world, if the kingdom of God is really in the world, if the power of God is really in the world, why then should the faithful suffer? Why then should those who believe in God continue to suffer, while those like Herod, who live in injustice, continue to be in power?

"Are you the one who is to come or are we to expect some other?" This happens so often in the world. In the middle of the 1850s, when slavery in the United States was still a reality, a black bishop, Bishop Nathanael Pole said: "If I were to believe that all this"—the suffering, the pain, the murder of black people in the United States— "was the will of God and that this had his approval, I should deny my faith and throw my Bible into the heart of the sea." I can understand that bishop.

I have seen this very often in the young people that I work with. I am sure that many of you have had experiences like this. What happens to you when you decide that you will give your life, all of your commitment and all that you have, for the struggle for peace and justice? What happens to you, when you refuse to accept this world as it is, and you decide that there must be a different world?

What happens is that you commit yourself to find that different world. You want that different life. But maybe that commitment breaks up relationships with friends or, even more difficult, it breaks up relationships with parents. I have often had to try to bring parents and children together when their relationship seemed permanently destroyed because of the commitment of the children to things that their parents never understood.

Much doubt rises up in our hearts when we realize that the struggle for justice, peace, and humanity has been going on for so long. I know there are young people who think that the struggle really begins when they enter into it. But there are also others who realize that we have been part of this struggle for many centuries now. I am quite overwhelmed with a deep and nameless sense of despair when I think that in my country we have been struggling with racism, inhumanity, hatred, and injustice for 332 years now. It seems that the powers of evil get stronger every day; they do not get weaker. The symbols of whatever is wrong in the world seem to be getting clearer every day. By this time

I would have thought that black people would have been a little closer to our liberation.

When the prime minister of South Africa travels to Europe and has luncheons all over the place, Europe is charmed and enchanted by the man. Even the pope receives him. What is this? The doubt then rises up in the hearts of people: "Why? How long, Lord?" That is their cry.

We had thought that four years of President Reagan in the United States would be quite enough for the next century to deal with. But now I fear that we may see another four years of the same man, and of the same policies, and of the same undermining of everything that is worthwhile in the world. I go into deep despair sometimes.

What Do We Do?

There is also the helplessness that one has to deal with in the face of all that happens in the world. What do we do about the continued destruction of people? What do we do about the continued disdain of the superpowers when it comes to the lives of people in the Pacific, for instance, where nuclear waste is already eating away at everything that they have, including their human dignity? What do we do about the continuing genocide of the Indian people in Guatemala? What do we do about the continuing assistance that is being given to unjust governments in Africa, in Asia, and in Latin America by the superpowers? What do we do about the untimely death of comrades and young warriors for justice in our struggle?

If you had stood on the streets of Soweto or elsewhere in South Africa in 1976 you would have seen how the police mercilessly shot down children who wanted nothing else but a different society with a future for themselves. You would have seen, as I did then, what happened to those children and to their parents knowing that the world did not even blink an eye, and that this made no difference to the world's relationship with the South African government. Seeing all this tempts one to ask: "Where in heaven or in God's name is this God that I am supposed to believe in?"

In 1980 when the school children in Cape Town refused to go to school and demonstrated against the apartheid system, the first boy who was shot down by the police was a boy by the name of Bernard Fortuin. He was ten years old, and he was sent by his mother to go and fetch his little brother, because his mother feared that the younger boy might get involved in what was happening on the streets. Somehow little Bernard got caught in the crowds, and he was shot down by the police. As he lay there on the street, his mother came running because someone had told her. She pushed her way through the crowd, and finally she was stopped by the barrier of policemen who hit at her with their clubs and their gunbutts. When she spoke to them, she said, "Please, this is my son, let me go to him! I want to be with him!" One policeman said to her the words that appeared, I think, in every newspaper in the world: "Let the bastard die."

When I tried to speak to Mrs. Fortuin two days before the funeral, I found myself speechless. I could not say anything at all. I found that my eleven years of theological training had not really equipped me for a moment like that. I was speechless also because I did not know how to deal with the anger and the doubt that were in my own heart about this God who allowed this to happen.

It is in moments like these that the question of John the Baptist becomes *the* question in the hearts of so many people in the world: "Are you the one who is to come or are we to expect some other?" Moments like these cause me to stop a little bit and to ask: is it worth it? Because one does become tired of this struggle. When this happens, too many doubts seem to be able to stop you dead in your tracks.

There is a poem I want to read to you which expresses so clearly what I sometimes feel and maybe you too feel sometimes. It is a poem by a Malaysian poet. It is a poem called "Radiation and the Rubaiyat":

> And yes, I too am
> tired of protest.
> O to be done
> with this madness
> and like Khayyam
> take to the wilderness
> with a loaf of bread
> a flask of wine
> a book of verse
> and a wild wild lass. . . .
>   But now beneath
> that nuclear
> bough, Omar,
> there's no paradise
> the bread crumbles
> to radio-active pieces

the wine is toxic
the maiden leukemic
a skeleton
screaming, not singing
in a wilderness of ash.
(Cecil Rajenda, *Songs for the Unsung* [WCC, 1983])

But still you feel that although you really want to run away, somehow there are things in this world which compel you to continue.

If we turn to Matthew 11 we find that Jesus listens to the disciples of John the Baptist. He sends them a message: "Go and tell John what you hear and see!" I want you to notice here that Jesus does not enter into some theological discourse on faith. He does not recommend that John read the books of a certain theologian before his head is chopped off. He does not even advise him to pray! He just tells the disciples: "You go and tell John what you hear and see."

In other words, he is pointing to God's actions in the Messiah. He is telling John to understand that something is happening in the world. Something is happening to the lives of people in the world. And whenever one has to deal with doubt, uncertainty, and despair, the thing to do is to notice what God is doing in the world, and to become a participant in the actions of God in the world.

What is Happening?

The blind see, the lame walk, the dead are raised up, lepers are cleansed, the deaf hear, and the poor have the gospel preached to them.

Let me share with you what I think this means for us today. One of the great difficulties we sometimes have, is simply to see that in the midst of the mayhem and suffering, in the midst of death, and in the midst of so much pain and injustice, there are signs of hope that God places in the world. Our blindness to God's action in the world and to the signs of hope makes it extremely difficult for us to understand what our own action ought to be.

When the blind begin to see, it means that God opens our eyes to see hope, to see possibilities for freedom, to see the action in which God is involved in the world. But it also means that we are to become people who understand that the words of those in power, with might and hatred and violence as their trademark, are not the last words in the world. They cannot really challenge the living One. In the end, the life of Jesus Christ, and therefore our life in Jesus Christ, will be the last word. We have to learn to see that.

When Elisha was fleeing from Dothan, he found when he woke up in the morning that the king had found out where he was and had sent his whole army to come and capture him. His servant discovered this first and panicked. He ran up to Elisha and said: "Look! Look! There are the armies of the king." But Elisha saw beyond the armies of the king—he also saw the armies of angels that the Lord had sent to protect him. So he said to his servant: "Do not be afraid, for those who are with us are more than those who are with them." Then he prayed and said: "Lord, open his eyes that he may see."

This is the kind of sight that we need, namely to see beyond Pershings and missiles, beyond might and power, and beyond decisions taken over our heads. God has placed possibilities for freedom, human action, love, and justice not beyond, but within our reach—if we will only see. And if we can see these possibilities, maybe we can then become involved in the possibilities to change the world.

The lame walk, Jesus says. Too many times people are paralyzed with fear and despair. We think that we are doomed to sit, that we are too lame to get up and walk. It is possible, Jesus says, if we have faith. We shall be strengthened, our legs will become strong, and we shall walk the path of righteousness and justice.

The dead are raised up. We, coming from Africa, believe that before a person dies physically, that person can die in numerous other ways too. This happens if you have no human relationship with other people, or if your humanity is not recognized, or if there can be no feeling of togetherness with other people, or if you are constantly rejected, or if you have to live outside of human communities, or if the other does not see you.

This is also the meaning of a greeting we have in one of the languages of my country. Normally you would translate it "good morning," but it really means "I see you"—I recognize in you my own humanity, and both of us will affirm that by our relationship. So when we say "lumela," it means "good morning"—but it really means "I see you." Without that living, affirming human relationship, you are dead.

I think that many of us have died because of inhumanity, dehumanization, and racism. So many of us have died because we were not accepted as human beings. But it is possible through the power of God that a dead person can be raised up, and we can become alive and affirm our humanity not only by saying "I am human" but also by acting like a human being who shall claim for himself or herself the gifts of God that are due to us.

The lepers are cleansed. I think this means that we are no longer rejected because we are accepted by God in Christ. Our human dignity cannot be taken away by any document from human hands.

The deaf hear. It is not true that we are doomed to die or that we are helpless or that we have no future. Once our eyes and ears have been opened, we know what it means when we say, "In Christ—the future is now." We may begin to act.

An Invitation to Action

All this, my friends, is an invitation to action. It is an invitation for you to look around you and see what God is doing in the world. It is an invitation to understand that doubt, fear, uncertainty, and despair can only be dispelled by our participation, by our believing, and by our actions with God in this world.

There may be very difficult days ahead. In my country there are young white people who have chosen justice and who now have become conscientious objectors. They refuse to go into South Africa's army because they refuse to kill another person for the sake of apartheid. They face going to jail for six years, but they look at me and say, "That's alright, because we know what we are doing."

For many there will be detention without trial, not only in my country, but maybe in yours as well. There may be torture in those jails. You may be banned.

There may even be the ugliness of physical death.

The threat of death sometimes causes great fear in the hearts of many people. I know that, and I have to struggle with that ever since I became aware of that threat for myself.

I will never forget one day—maybe three years ago—a man came to our door to explain to me that he had been in prayer and fasting for three days, and that God had revealed to him who the real enemies of God were in the country. God had appointed him as my executioner. He was a big man, and all the while I thought, "When is this man going to pull out his gun?" But having given me his warning, he left. As I closed the door, my little boy, who was then three years old, came running up the hallway, and as I held him I realized for the first time in my life what all of this could mean.

I do not mind admitting to you that it was a very difficult time for me then. I found that when I prayed, I had to pray out loud to make my commitment to God, my commitment not to stop or to falter, but to continue to be able to do what I believed was right. I had to pray out loud because I was afraid that if I did not hear my own voice, I might go back on my commitment.

Through all of this one needs to know, to see, to find the strength to walk, to hear words of hope, to see signs of God's love and action in the world so that one may become a participant.

Let me end with a word of Paul to the Romans which has come to mean so much to so many of us: "But I am assured that neither life nor death, nor principalities, nor powers, nor height, nor depth, nor any creature can separate us from the love of God which is in Jesus Christ, our Lord."

God bless you!

8

I Have Seen a Land

Brothers and sisters, ladies and gentlemen, friends and enemies—I can't believe that everyone here is a friend, and I would not like to leave anyone out—so please feel welcome.

There is a group of people here tonight who work for the South African Television (and I need to say that) who wanted me to speak to them so that they could get me on film and show me to the nation. The last time they did that was when I was in Durban visiting the six people in the consulate there. I came out, and we had a press conference, and I spoke. When I got home, my little girl, Pulani, who is the cheekiest of all my children—showing very clearly that she does not take after her father—said to me, "Daddy, they didn't let you say anything on TV." I said to her, "Baby, that is the problem with the South African Television. They don't want to let you say anything, unless you say what they want you to say, and they like it then." And I just want to make very sure that everybody understands. I don't hate these people; I don't have time for that—I have too much on my plate these days, more than ever before. But I'd like very much to say that the policy of the United Democratic Front is clear and correct. As long as we do not get a clear and solemn understanding that we will be given clear and impartial coverage so that the people of South Africa can see and hear for themselves what we are and what we stand for and what we want and what we think of this country, we will not allow them here. I will go and I will speak with the people in the South African Television if it can be live and if it is for no less than ten minutes. They can ask me any question they want—but I will not go and have a little interview and be clipped or whatever it is that they call it, so that I am not even recognizable.

And so, now that we are all welcome—let's get down to serious business. The minister has ordered that I be charged under Section 27

In a public meeting of the UDF in Cape Town on November 26, 1984, Allan Boesak answered the charges made against him by the Minister of Law and Order, Louis Le Grange.

of the Police Act. There are people who thought that I had been detained, because when you hear "Section" in this country. . . .

He has also said that he has now ordered the police to open a dossier on me. I was a little disappointed, I must say. I had thought that they had dossiers from way back when—now I know that they only started two weeks ago.

Section 27 says: "Any person who publicizes any untrue matter in relation to any member of the force, when that force member or the force itself is functioning, without having reasonable grounds that that statement is true, shall be guilty of an offense . . . da . . . da . . . da. . . ." And then they tell you there is a fine of up to R10,000 or five years in jail or both.

Now, what angered the minister is apparently what I had said on a visit to Australia. (If you want to be famous, go to Australia!) There I had an interview with a person who asked me what I thought about what was happening in South Africa. Among other things, we talked about the unrest of the last three months; we talked about the campaign of the United Democratic Front and other organizations to get people to stay away from the polls; we talked about the success of all of that; and we talked about the meaning of what we were seeing in South Africa. "What does it mean," he asked me, "when seven thousand troops are asked to go into—or ordered to go into—the townships?" And I said that that means that we have an undeclared state of civil war.

I thought it was clear and honest and I thought it was simply saying what I saw was the truth. The minister is upset about that. He is even more upset because I talked about the role of the military and of the South African Defense Force, and I said that we know that they are committing unbelievable atrocities in the townships. I mentioned only one example of that—the example of the little boy who was shot in both legs by a policeman. That story was told to us by the people we visited as a delegation of the South African Council of Churches in Sebokeng in September.

I do not know whether the minister knows what an atrocity is. I have looked it up. It is, it says, a repellent deed, an inhuman act. Something that offends ordinary human decency. An act that is inexcusable and ought not to be defended. When I hear or when I read of a little boy three years old who was playing in the yard with his friends and who was shot dead by the police while he was playing in his yard, then I think that that is an atrocity. And if it is true I will say it.

Then I hear that little Thabo Sibeko, six years old, who was sitting on the front stoop of his home, playing with other children, was shot there on his front stoop so that he died as he went into the house, crying for his mother! Six years old! And I ask myself what kind of threat could he have been to any policeman? I think that that is an unbelievable atrocity. It should not have happened. If the minister does not know that, then he must go into those townships and speak to those people. Or if he does not know it now, I am almost tempted to say then may the day come that he will experience it and know what it means— he will never again say that that is not an atrocity.

It is very clear that either he does not know or he does not want to know what his police are doing in the townships. And if he does not know, and if he does not want to know, he should not be the minister. He should not be in the government, and in fact not only should he not be the minister, the government shouldn't be the government at all.

I wonder what you expect when you let the police and the army move into the townships and then you order a blackout on all news. The press is not allowed to go in there; the press is not allowed to monitor the situation, to come and report what they see and what they have experienced. What do you think will happen when there is no possibility for public scrutiny of what the police and the military are doing. What do you imagine is happening when there is no public accountability from the police and from the military for what they are doing in the townships. For when you move against defenseless people, and you move in with full military preparedness, armed to the teeth, what do you think is going to happen when you let these people loose on defenseless civilians and on children, especially when the thing that they have been trained for in the army—the only thing that they have been trained for in the army—is to kill as efficiently as possible. We don't think about that, but when we take a person from civilian life and we make him into a soldier, the one thing that we train him for is to kill efficiently. That is what soldiers do, you know. And when they move into the townships and there is no control or there is no possibility of control, then of course you must prepare yourselves that things will happen that you would not like to happen.

But when those things happen you must not try to make the people who talk about it out to be liars and slanderers of the country. You must rather try to find out whether it is true. This the minister has not been willing to do. I think that that is wrong, and I think that the South

African public and our people have a right to know what is happening in the townships. You cannot say that because SABC TV does not show it—it does not happen. You cannot say that because the press is prohibited from publishing everything—it doesn't happen. I have said so before and I will say it again. The whole world saw on their television screens how South African policemen beat men and women and children who had done nothing. They saw what happened on August 27 in Lenasia and in other townships. They saw since then what has happened, especially during the first month of the unrest in the townships in the Vaal triangle and on the East Rand.

Now this government has made laws which make it well-nigh impossible for the press to report these things. They have made laws which protect the military, which protect the police, like this Section 27 of the Police Act. They have indemnity laws so that it is almost impossible for us as ordinary people to get to the truth and to say, "This is actually what happened."

There is an all-pervading atmosphere of violence and of threat and of intimidation so that even those people who have suffered under the violence of the police sometimes are too afraid to come out and testify to it. Apartheid is a violent system; we have said so often before. It is a system that can only be maintained by ongoing violence, by wanton violence. It is a system that would not survive for one single moment if there were no police force or if there were no army, if there were no violent reaction from the government every single time the people protest. In every police state the police and the army are not really instruments at the service of all of the people, because they become the instruments of the most vicious kind of oppression to maintain the position of power of those who see themselves as the powerful group. And this police state is no exception.

This is what we have seen, over the last three months. And again when we read these things that have happened to our people, and when you read what happens to people like little Thabo Sibeko, the question for me is not only, "What kind of mentality does a policeman have who will pick up a gun and shoot a six year old in the back?" but the question is ultimately and finally, "What kind of climate has been created in a country where such a thing is actually possible—where a policeman can do it and get away with it?" *That* is the question that we have to ask.

And so the responsibility for the violence that we have to live with every day, the responsibility for the violence that is systemic—built into the system of apartheid—the responsibility for making it impossible for people to really work for peace without the threat of death—that responsibility I lay squarely at the door of the South African government. They are responsible and they must be told this, and I will tell them so long as God gives me breath in my body. I recognize that it is the responsibility of the minister to protect his police force, but I must also say that it is my responsibility to protect my people. And I will not allow these things to happen when I know about them and I am being told about them by the very mothers and fathers who have seen their children die, and keep quiet about it. If I hear it, the world will know it as long as I can speak. And I want you to remember that that is your responsibility as well.

The responsibility to defend those who are defenseless, to speak for those who are voiceless, to make sure that the world understands what is happening, and to make sure that we in this country are aware of what is happening, is not only the responsibility of one or two people. It is our joint responsibility.

Because I have done this, the minister has called me a liar and a slanderer. He must take responsibility for those words. I have in my possession affidavits, and I will read simply a few examples of what has happened to people during the last few months since the police and the military invaded the townships and since we have had this unrest.

There was a little boy called Walter Pule Makhata, a schoolboy aged fourteen from Naledi, Soweto. He went to the shop to buy a loaf of bread, was hit by birdshot and found dead.

In Katlehong, three children, one of them mentally retarded, were allegedly assaulted by police on September 13, 1984. The police fired tear gas into the house and walked in, asking where the children were. When they found them, they started to kick and hit them all over their bodies. This happened to children. This is from an SACC affidavit. Who is the liar, Mr. Le Grange?

On Friday, September 28, the horrendous example (that the Reverend Chicane has quoted) of the young boy who was shot in the police van by the policeman. His name is Jacob Moleleke.

On August 15 an unnamed boy (he refused to give his name, but called himself A.B.), aged fifteen, was on the roof of his house in Watville, Benoni, with two other people making repairs. There were no apparent disturbances in the area at that time. Then the police came through shooting tear-gas cylinders. Some people ran from the street into A.B.'s house for shelter. The other two men on the roof fled but he lay down on the roof. A policeman mounted the ladder to the roof, came up to him and discharged a tear-gas cylinder into his face. He has lost his left eye as a result. Another SACC affidavit. If this is not an atrocity, what is? And if the minister does not know it, he must make it his business to know it.

Nicholas Mldulwa, ten years old, was sent out by his father one evening to fetch firewood. The area was so quiet that his father actually thought this was safe to do. A Combi came by, a shot was fired. The father ran out and found his boy hit on the left side of his forehead with a rubber bullet. The police came and told him to keep the matter quiet. He refused, went to the lawyers, and he signed an affidavit. He even gave the registration number of the vehicle: EDY549B.

Elsie Nana, nineteen years old, was arrested on October 3 while attending a prayer vigil. She was told to write a statement and give details about whatever she knew about the activities of other people. When she told them she was two months pregnant, she was assaulted— repeatedly kicked and hit with a sjamboc [a rubber baton] on her stomach.

All of this the minister can ask of the people who have made these affidavits. All I want to ask him is, *"Who is the Liar?* Who is the slanderer? Who is the one who is trying to cover up deeds like these?" As long as these things happen and as long as we hear about it, it will be our responsibility to testify against the evil that is gripping this country.

We will not be silent. We will not stop doing this. We will refuse to be intimidated. It seems to me that the South African government thinks that these things that happen, these atrocities—yes, *atrocities,* Mr. Minister!—will stop us from demanding our freedom. But the South African government must learn that the time that they can avert change, fundamental change, in South Africa by merely reaching for a gun is over. We will no longer be silenced by fear, or by intimidation, or even by the wanton killing of our people. The demands are there, and are clear. Release the political prisoners; unban the organizations; scrap all these laws that have made South Africa a hell for so many people to live in; stop killing our children and our people on the streets; let us participate in an open democratic society—then there will be peace in this country, and they must know that.

And so the state threatens to ban the organizations, and they threaten to ban the United Democratic Front. It will be a little difficult, because the UDF, I have often said, is the people of South Africa, and they cannot ban the people. The UDF embodies the dreams of the people of South Africa, and they cannot ban that dream. The UDF embodies the aspirations of the people toward a free and just society, and they cannot ban that. They can do whatever they want, but the determination of our people to be free will remain and will become the real reality that even Mr. Le Grange and his government will have to face. And so it seems to me that all of the threats will not really in the end help the South African government.

There are threats against individuals, and I do not know what the minister has in mind for me. I have just heard that I will be charged. Over the last week or so the threats to my life have come in more frequently than before. Someone has called me up and said the system has many ways to get at you, and they will do that. I do not know what he means, I do not understand, but it does not matter now. That is no longer the most important thing in my life.

The most important thing is what I want you to remember tonight: what we are fighting for, what we are struggling for. What our people are suffering for, what our people are dying for—that is worthwhile. Let us not give that up. Let us remember that no threat and no form of intimidation and no trick that the system can play on any one of us, including myself, can bring us to the point where we will be silenced, where we will accept the situation as it is, because if we do that we might as well give up and die. We sometimes die a thousand times before we die, because when we are afraid we die every day a little bit. We die in our humanity, we die in our determination, and we die in our self-respect. Let us not come to that point.

For me, it is clear I have experienced in this last year something within the community of the UDF that will remain with me as long as I live. I have experienced support, and I have experienced a determination, and I have experienced a love for freedom that is a precious gift that we have. We must not give that up, and this is what we have to continue to work for. I have seen a new South Africa. I have seen a land not of apartheid; not of death; not of chains; but a land of joy and a land of freedom and a land of peace. Let us fight for that land.

And I have seen a new land where our children will no longer be bowed down by the yoke of racism. Let us fight for that land.

I have seen a land where our people shall work and enjoy the fruits of their labor. Let us fight for that land.

I have seen a land where families will no longer be broken up and where mothers and fathers will enjoy the love and the respect of their children. Let us fight for that land.

I have seen a land where the misery of relocation is no more, and where the graves dug for little children who will tomorrow die of hunger remain empty. Let us fight for that land.

I have seen a land where those of us who fight for freedom, and for justice and for the self-respect of this country will no longer be sent to prison, will no longer be tortured, will no longer be threatened, will no longer be shot on the streets of our nation, but will be rewarded with honor and with the presence of justice. Let us fight for that land.

And I have seen a land where we, together, will build something that is worthwhile, that is faithful to what we believe. Let us not give that up, but make tonight a new dedication for that moment. Because I believe it does not matter what happens now. I believe that the freedom that we have struggled for, and the freedom that we have died for, will become a reality. *You* can make it happen. God bless you!

9

If This Is Treason, I Am Guilty

I bring you greetings from the president and the people of Mozambique. I visited there recently, and the most significant thing on that trip which was made clear to me is that the minds and the hearts of the people of Mozambique have not changed, that their own commitment to the struggle in spite of what has happened is clear, and that they shall continue to seek ways and means to support, as much as possible, our own people in our struggle for liberation.

I think it is absolutely crucial for us to understand the meaning of this, given the difficulties that the people of Mozambique are facing right now. The visit that I made to Mozambique and my discussions with government leaders there were really geared to this one fact that we should all know: nothing, they told me, has broken the solidarity that they feel with us. I have been there. I have *seen* the evidence of that solidarity. We should not allow the South African government with whatever trick it may think up to bring division between the people of South Africa and the people of Mozambique, or for that matter between the people of South Africa and the people of any frontline country.

We have entered a decisive phase in our struggle. Those of us who have warned that the South African government cannot be trusted, that the reforms that they are talking about are cosmetic, that apartheid and racism still reign supreme, and that the South African government still has only one goal, namely absolute power for itself and for the white minority and continued control over the majority of our people in this country, were right. Subsequent events since we have begun to make this clear have shown that this government indeed cannot be trusted. While the South African government talked of reforms and while they were engaged in a massive effort to mislead the international commu-

This speech was given at a gathering of the UDF in Durban, February 27, 1985.

nity, they instituted a racist constitution. While they were talking about reform they continued the homelands policy. While they were talking about reform they continued the denationalization of South Africa's people, robbing our black people of their birthright and of their right to stay in this land. While they were talking about reforms they continued their forced removals, their policies of subtle genocide by forcing our people from the lands where they had lived for so many years into those concentration camps the South African government calls relocation areas. While they were talking about reform and while they were signing peace treaties with countries like Mozambique, they detained us, they shot at our people, they tear-gassed us when we peacefully, so powerfully demonstrated our rejection of their policies and of their constitution. While they were talking about peace with other nations they sent their police and their troops into our townships, they broke up our funeral services with violence, they threatened our unarmed people, and they murdered our children on the streets of the townships. While they were talking about reform and while they were lying to the world saying that apartheid is dead, the unrest all over the country proved that the struggle for justice and our struggle for genuine liberation shall continue. The boycott not only proved the discontent of our people but also proved the determination of our people. And these are the things that the South African government cannot even begin to understand or begin to stop. While they spouted their propaganda across the world we proved to the world and to the government that neither smear campaigns nor dogs nor guns nor tear gas can undermine the determination of our people to be free.

So now the South African government is in trouble. They don't know what to do. There is no direction, there is no sense of where they are going. If you go and ask the people who sit in parliament what it is that they want before the end of this year, no one will be able to tell you, because they don't know what they want. There is such a state of confusion that one is justified in saying that not since Sharpeville in 1960 was the South African government so vulnerable to pressure, so confused, as now. There is no control over the economy—and you know the reason the rand is so low is that it has become so expensive to live abroad these days.

So they are worried because they have this new constitution, and with all their pomp and splendor they have opened the new parliament. Now they have their three "parliaments": they have the whites on one side, and they have the coloreds on another side, and they have the Indians on another side. And the thing is not working—and that is the problem of course. While they are there they are supposed to govern this country. They are supposed to take note of what is happening, and they are supposed to think about this and to make intelligent noises about what is happening. They are supposed to see the problems of our country, and to try to find solutions because that is what they are there for—so they say. Indeed you know the problems facing South Africa. We have unrest in this land that has not stopped since it began in the middle of 1984. There is a rising cost of living that cannot be stopped by the government either: the general sales tax will go up, essential subsidies will be dropped, the salaries of the new MP's will have to be paid, their new homes will have to be paid for. There is a tax relief for the rich—you saw that in the newspapers the other day, didn't you? They were supposed to pay extra tax on all those perks that they have— all those expensive cars, and homes, and things—and the government said "Oh no, Oh no, this is very difficult, and we can't do that. We will have to wait a few years to implement this policy." Who do you think is going to pay the eight hundred million rand that the South African government is losing because the rich are not going to be taxed? *You* are going to pay it, the people will have to pay it. This is not something that is being discussed. Crossroads is burning—eighteen people are dead. The war in Namibia continues—three million rand a day is spent on the government's illegal occupation of that country they should have been out of long ago. They are not discussing that.

Here in our own land there is a crisis in education. Our children are not going to school—and there are very good reasons for that—but they are not talking about that. What are they talking about? You saw in the newspapers: the thing they are discussing is the case of those white MP's who may or may not have had a Hottentot for a grandfather some time. That is what they are talking about. And in the middle of this bankruptcy, the state president makes an announcement—although not for our consumption, because we know the government and we don't believe them even when they say these things; this is for the United States and for Britain. The state president says, "From now on the government will actually recognize that there will be a permanent presence of black people in the urban areas." We can now actually live in South Africa. That is what they say. "And therefore there will be a cabinet committee who will look into the possibilities of these black people being able to participate in the affairs of the government within the framework of the new constitution." That is a long sentence, but it comes from the state president.

I want, publicly again, to ask the question, "If the state president makes the announcement that black people can actually live in South Africa now and the government will recognize them, what does he expect us to think?" They actually expect us to sit back and be very happy and be very grateful and to say "Ja, dankie baas . . ." [Yes, thank you, boss]. Doesn't he know that black people have been here long before he came here, that black people belong in this country, and that we will be here long after he goes back, and doesn't he know that this land is not his to give us—that this land is ours and will one day again belong to us?

We are not grateful for these little concessions that they make. We are merely saying to the state president and to his government, do not fool yourselves now. Don't go around trying to fool the world, because certainly you cannot fool us—we know where we belong!

The problem that we have to face is how we can in this situation keep the initiative that we have gained. The fact is that international pressure is growing; in the United States, in spite of constructive engagement—maybe also because of constructive engagement—there is an unprecedented movement of protest against the South African government and its policies and against constructive engagement. Never before have people in the U.S. been so engaged in solidarity with the people of South Africa. And this will happen again and again and again. They are engaged in the struggle not simply because they feel like it, but because you, the people of South Africa, are engaged in the struggle, and you have made them see that it is worthwhile for them to throw their weight behind us. And that is important.

All over Europe the movement against apartheid is growing. I spoke not so long ago to a new organization called Western European Parliamentarians for Action against Apartheid, and they have pledged themselves to try to put pressure on their own governments and through them to put as much pressure as possible on the South African government so that fundamental change can take place. These people are doing that because in South Africa there are people who believe in the struggle, who fight for what we believe in, who believe in justice, who believe in liberation, and who believe that we ought to be participating in that struggle. As long as you are involved, the people of the world

will more and more become involved. To the chagrin of the South
African government, President Kaunda goes around the world and asks
for pressure on the South African government and calls for disinvest-
ment. The Danish government this morning announced that it will no
longer allow its companies to bring new investment to South Africa.
You see, the campaign is working.

In response to this unprecedented international pressure the South
African government is trying to show that it is really changing, so they
say that Nelson Mandela can come out of jail and that Walter Sisulu
can come out of jail. But while they say to Walter Sisulu, "Please come
out of jail" and to Nelson Mandela, "Please come out of jail," they
take Sisulu's wife and put her in prison. And they take fifteen other
people and put them in prison. What is the matter with this government?
You know, our problem in this country is really that we sit with a
government that can only think so far. There must really be people in
that government who cannot think very well. One wonders where they
went to school; if we knew, we could go talk to those schools and say,
"If you turn out any further governments for this country, please advise
us."

I noticed something when the government made Nelson Mandela the
offer of release. A magazine in this country wrote that Mandela should
accept that offer because in doing so he would not endear himself to
the people who now want to claim him—like the United Democratic
Front. He would instead establish his credibility with all the peace-
loving, thinking people in South Africa, namely "them." I read that
article and I thought, what a cheek! Who are they to now claim Mandela
for themselves? They are the ones who created policies which made it
impossible for black people to live in this country like decent human
beings. They are the ones who, when we started to resist these policies,
made laws that made it impossible for us even to take the first step of
saying, "This is our situation; this is our land; we want to live here as
people recognized as citizens." Then they banned his organization, they
drove him to violence, they locked him up for twenty-two years, they
banned and banished his wife, they locked up in Robben Island and the
prisons of this country the people who worked with him, they called
him a terrorist, they called him a communist—and now, when they are
in difficulty, they want to offer him a conditional release and say that
we must not claim him because he must establish his credibility with
them. Mandela does not need to establish his credibility with those

people. Mandela does not need to establish his credibility with anyone but the people who are still in the struggle for justice and liberation in this country, and that's you. And he doesn't need to establish his credibility with you.

But of course, since the South African government is facing all this difficulty, someone has to get the blame. This time it is the turn of the United Democratic Front. Mr. Le Grange made a speech last night. As usual, it was a speech that was full of threats, and intimidation, and promises of more intimidation. And he singled out, again, the United Democratic Front as an organization that is creating a climate of revolution in South Africa. I want to say to Mr. Le Grange: "Mr. Le Grange, I am actually getting a little sick and tired of all these threats. The people of South Africa are getting a little tired of these threats. We are engaged in a struggle for liberation, not because we want to die, but because we want our people to be free. We are engaged in a struggle for liberation, not because we wish to die, but because you oppress us, and as long as you continue to oppress us we will have to resist. We are people, and we are people who belong in this land. The climate of revolution, Mr. Minister, is not created by those who struggle for justice and peace, but the climate of revolution in this country is created by those who make policies that despise and undermine the human dignity of people. The climate of revolution is created by those who make policies that exploit our people, that take away the necessities of the many to give luxuries to the few. The climate of revolution is created by those who make policies that create hunger and starvation in the homelands while the tables of the rich in white South Africa are sagging with food that will be thrown into the dustbin. The climate of revolution is not created by the United Democratic Front, but by those people like you, Mr. Le Grange, who refuse to listen to the voice of reason, who refuse to listen to our people when they say we want our rights, and we want them here, and we want them now, because they are our rights. The climate of revolution is not created by the United Democratic Front, but by those people like you, Mr. Le Grange, who detain without trial; by those who allow our people to be tortured in their jails; by those who allow the wanton killing of our people on the streets of our nation." These are the things that are creating a climate of revolution in our nation, and Mr. Le Grange must not blame the United Democratic Front—he must put the blame where it belongs,

right in front of the door of the South African government, of which
he is a part.

Now the government has charged some of our brothers and sisters
with treason. As I have said over and over again tonight, this is a
serious charge. Treason is described as organizing, or taking part in,
or instigating, armed revolt in order to overthrow the government.
Actually, they are being charged under a section of the Internal Security
Act in which any act of subversion—which can include speaking out
against the South African government or calling for pressure on the
South African government—is also treason. It is wide, it is irrespon-
sible, but it is a law that is on the statute books of this country. So these
people will be charged with treason.

I want to say that I consider this a scandalous, dastardly, and cow-
ardly act. I have worked for a long time with the people who are being
charged. I have not heard them call for violence. From its inception,
the United Democratic Front has been an organization committed to
nonviolence. Under the most difficult circumstances, we did not ask
people to take up arms. We said to our people, let us find ways and
means, with all of the odds against us, even at this late hour, to try
peacefully to express our legitimate political aspirations in this country.

We know that we have had a long battle behind us. We know that
every single effort toward peaceful change in this country has been met
by the government with violence and ended by a massacre. We know
how our people marched peacefully on March 21 now twenty-five years
ago in Sharpeville. One day soon we shall be commemorating that
tragic event, when their peaceful demonstration ended in bloodshed,
most of them shot in the back. We know that in 1976 our children took
to the streets with nothing in their hands except placards which said to
the South African police, "We do not want to fight. Please release our
comrades and our friends." Those children were shot down by the police
by the hundreds. And we know that in 1980 in Cape Town our children
took up the challenge and marched peacefully for a better future for
themselves, expressing only that they do not want to grow up in a
country where racism is rife, and where oppression is the order of the
day, and where exploitation is around every corner, and where our
people are being pushed into little holes in the homelands where they
will die of hunger and despair. The answer the South African government gave once again was guns, and dogs, and tear gas—and our
children died. And you will remember that when little Bernard Fortuin,

ten years old, was shot on the streets of Elsies River, lying there bleeding to death, his mother wanted to talk to him. But they refused, and they shoved her away with their gun butts, and when she said to the policeman, "Please! He is my son," he said the words that reverberated around the world, to the shame of South Africa: "Let the bastard die!" You know that.

And now in 1984, we have formed the United Democratic Front and have said to people, "Let us not despair; let us not say that the only answer to the South African government's violence is violence; let us not seek to repay them with the same things that they are doing to us; let us not seek to be overcome with evil, but indeed to find a way to overcome evil with good by peacefully demonstrating what it is that we want." We made this organization into a force that even the whole world will now have to reckon with. We never picked up a single stone, but they came again with their dogs and their guns and their bazookas, and they killed our people even on the night of the election. We in the United Democratic Front said, "Let us try to find ways of telling our young people to commit themselves once again, even now, to a strategy of nonviolence." And we did, and the world respects the United Democratic Front for it. It was the South African government who turned around and detained our people. It was the South African government who turned around and sent their police to our demonstrations on the night of the election, and it was they who started again to shoot at our people. What is it that we have done? We in the United Democratic Front have created a unity that this country has not seen for almost three decades. We brought back the spirit of the struggle that we knew in the 1950s. We were the people who were able to bring people together even in this racist land—where hatred is the order of the day because hatred is the theme of the South African government—to make it possible for black and white to work together in the face of strong criticism from others. We have been able to say to people: "Do not look at the matter simply by the color of a person's skin, but try to judge that person in terms of that person's commitment to the struggle for justice and liberation." And we have succeeded in doing that.

In one single year, in a short twelve-month period, we have brought together a mass movement now representing millions of people in this land. We have challenged the South African government's constitution, and what is more, we have won. We have made people aware of their rights in South Africa. We thereby exposed the violent, oppressive nature of this government. We have given the people of this land back their self-respect, we have given them a faith in the justice of our struggle, we have given them a belief that we shall overcome. This is the United Democratic Front. We stand for things that the South African government cannot understand. We stand for democracy. They don't know the meaning of the word. We stand for nonracialism. They cannot stand it when people of different races can live and work together. We stand for an open democratic society. They cannot stand it, because then they know that their violence will have come to an end.

But there is something more. We must ask the question, is what we have done treason? I, brothers and sisters, have called for the foundation and the formation of the United Democratic Front. I have spoken more than anybody else over the last year. I have said publicly that apartheid is evil, that it is a blasphemy, that it is a heresy. I have said that the South African government is unjust. I have said that this government is undemocratic, it is unrepresentative, it does not have the love or the support of the people, it has no right to exist, it is illegitimate, it should not be there. I have said openly that the South African government is a violent government. I have called for Christians and people of other faiths to pray for the downfall of the South African government, to pray that God should give us another government, to pray that God should remove them. I have from the very beginning resisted this government on the basis of my Christian commitment and of my Christian faith. And I shall continue to do so as long as God gives me breath in my body. If this is treason, then I am guilty of treason, and I would say to the South African government tonight, if I am guilty of treason, then charge me with treason and put me in jail.

I say this, brothers and sisters, not out of a sense of bravado. I have no desire to be a martyr—God knows my life for the last month or two has been hell enough. I say this not out of defiance, because I know that the minister to whom I am speaking now is a very powerful man, a man without a conscience who can do whatever he likes and get away with it. But I say this because in a perverted, unjust, and cruel society such as ours, where those who fight for freedom and peace and human dignity are banned, detained, and charged with treason while criminals sit in Parliament and receive accolades from those who share in their power and privilege, this is the only decent thing to do. And if I have committed treason by resisting the South African government—which is exactly what our brothers and sisters who are now in jail have done—

the South African government must now put me in jail and charge me with treason.

But you must know that we are indeed in the beginning of a decisive phase of our struggle in the history of our land. This is the beginning of the end of apartheid. Their days are numbered. And what you must do, Mr. Le Grange, you must do quickly, for your day of judgment is near. You must remember that the struggle does not depend on one or two or three or four people, and that the strength of the United Democratic Front has always been that we do not simply depend on those people that we have put in positions of leadership. The strength of the United Democratic Front has always been the people, has always been your commitment, has always been your participation in the struggle. So in the end it is not a question of whether the UDF will survive the onslaught because a few of the leaders are in jail facing trial, but in the end it is a question of whether you in your own commitment will remain faithful. I say to you my people tonight, do not begin to fear the future, do not begin to give up faith in our struggle and in the justice of our cause. Do not be overcome by the evil that this government represents, but overcome evil with good.

So in the midst of trial and tribulation I exhort you to remain a faithful people. In the midst of hopelessness and despair that sometimes overcomes us because we think that the powers standing over against us are so invincible, remain a hopeful people. In the midst of fear and uncertainties that come up in our own hearts because we do not know what tomorrow will bring, and we do not exactly know what will happen to us inside those jails or whether we will even come out alive, be a strong people. In the midst of unfaithfulness by so many who turn around and for a mess of pottage sell the birthright of our people just to sit in a bogus parliament and be given power and be given honor by people who do not even know the meaning of the words, be a committed people. And in the midst of the violence of this South African government which shall continue and which shall increase because they have created the monster that in the end is destined to devour even themselves, in the midst of the destruction that may come, remain a peace-loving people. In the midst of the madness of racism and hatred that still reign in this country, be a compassionate people. And in the end, if we remain faithful, if we take the risks that are necessary, and if we remain committed to what we believe in, we will be also a victorious people. God bless you!

10

In the Name of Jesus

My dear brothers and sisters, before I begin my sermon allow me to express our deep-felt thanks and appreciation to those churches which have taken decisions to support the call of the South African Council of Churches for this special service to pray for the removal of unjust rule in South Africa. There are not many issues that have raised so much controversy, so much pain, and so much division. In the face of such pressure these churches have stood firmly—we thank you. We also thank the individual ministers who are here today, those whose churches have not expressed themselves, even those whose churches through their leadership have expressed themselves clearly against this service. I need to tell you that today services are being held in many countries overseas, in the United States of America, in Europe, and in Canada; Christians are joining us in this prayer for the removal of unjust rule and for the establishment of God's own justice.

I take as my text Acts chapter 4, verses 9, 10, and 12.

If we are being called to account today for an act of kindness shown to a cripple and are asked how he was healed, then know this, you and everyone else in Israel, it is by the name of Jesus Christ of Nazareth whom you crucified but whom God raised from the dead that this man stands before you completely healed. Salvation is found in no one else, for there is no other name under heaven given to us, by which we must be saved.

Brothers and sisters, people of God, we are still in the season of Pentecost, and this reminds us of the outpouring of God's power in the Holy Spirit, the empowerment of God's people so that we are lifted up, raised up as it were, strengthened to fear no longer, to look no longer over our shoulder with anxiety, to ask no longer what shall happen to us if we dare speak or if we are known as followers of Jesus. We are raised up to enjoy the freedom and the fearlessness of the children of

On June 16, 1985, the ninth anniversary of the Soweto uprising, the SACC held in Cape Town a Service of Prayer for the End to Unjust Rule. Allan Boesak preached this sermon on that occasion.

God, for all those who know the empowerment of the Spirit will no longer bow under the threat of intimidation or under fear. Those who know the power of the Spirit of God will no longer watch anxiously or ask anxiously, "What will happen to me?" but will only ask, "What is it, Lord, that you want me to do?"

So with Pentecost the people are challenged and changed. We read of thousands of conversions. But something more happens; society and the world are disturbed and transformed, everybody knows that something extraordinary is happening. You can see how wonderful it is that God is working in the world, for then, and this is inevitable, comes the confrontation with the powers that be.

If people are being changed, if the structures of the world are being confronted, if the very world itself is faced with the challenge to be transformed, then no longer hatred but love shall rule, no longer fear but boldness shall rule, no longer injustice but justice shall rule. Powers which are built upon injustice must be ended, but these powers get upset and disturbed, they get angry, and so they call the apostles to account. They want to know what is happening here, "By what name, by what power are you doing this?" Chapters 3, 4, and 5 of Acts tell us, my brothers and sisters, how this drama unfolds.

First the church is very hesitant. Quietly Peter and John put the case. They do not want to be too direct; they say, "You must judge for yourselves, you must make your own decisions whether it is right in God's sight to obey yourself rather than God." As the situation develops, as the confrontation grows, and as the challenge can no longer be avoided both on the side of the powers and on the side of the apostles, a new answer comes. We hear the church pray, "Now, Lord, consider the oppressed and enable your servants to speak your word with great boldness." Later it is even more clear, much more poignant and indeed unequivocal: "We must obey God more than man," and so what you do to us is *your* decision; if you want to throw us in jail it is *your* decision; if you want to give us into the hands of the Romans in order to be killed as you killed Jesus it is *your* decision. However, as far as we are concerned, "We must obey God more than man."

This is the key verse, my brothers and sisters. It is this verse which rings like a bell in the history of the Christian church whenever it is faced with persecution. It is a verse that has people lifted up, ordinary, weak, human beings, and makes them stand firm and say with Martin Luther, "Here I stand. I can do no other." It is the verse that comes

after all that John Calvin said in his books in all the long chapters he
wrote about the Christian attitude toward the state and the government
and those in authority. After he has said, "Yes, we must obey them,"
"Yes, they are not bad by nature," "Yes, they might be good," "Yes,
we must listen to them," "Yes, we must trust them," "Yes, we must
help them." After all this he says, "But you must remember before all
else—we are called to obey God more than man."

However, this verse must and can only be understood in the light of
the portion that we have read: "There is no other name given under
heaven by which there is salvation, and you must know that what we
do we do in the name of Jesus Christ of Nazareth whom you have killed
and God has raised up from the dead." This is the basis of Christian
faith and Christian obedience. It is the foundation of the risk that Christians must take in the world, the foundation of all action by Christians
in the world. By what power, by what name, do you do this? There is
only one answer: "In the name of Jesus of Nazareth." Note here, my
brothers and sisters, that Peter, as he does so often in chapters 2, 3,
4, and 5 of Acts, says to these people, "the one you have crucified."
This is not an anti-Semitic challenge justifying discrimination against
the Jewish community for having killed Jesus. "No," Peter says, "you
must understand that you thought that he was dead but God has raised
him up and he is alive *now,* and his name is alive. You thought that you
had disposed of him, but he is alive and his name is a source of power
and inspiration for his people who believe in him."

This name, this name of Jesus, what name is this? It is the same
name Moses heard that day when he stood in the desert and watched
the flame devouring the bush, yet the flame would not go out. It is the
name of the God of the Exodus, it is the name of the God who told us,
"I am what I am; I am there for my people; I have heard their cry and
I have seen their suffering, how they are bent low under the whip,
under the yoke of slavery in Egypt. Therefore I shall come down and
deliver them from the hands of the king of Egypt." In this name Moses
challenged Pharaoh and told him in no uncertain terms, "Let my people
go." It is the same name Moses evoked when the people of Israel saw
the sea parting so they could walk through it. It is the same name under
which Israel marched through the wilderness, the fire by night and the
cloud by day to guide them. When they were hungry it was *that* name
which gave them food, and when they were thirsty it was *that* name
which gave them water. It was in the name of God that the prophets

took up, so clearly, the cause of the poor, the weak, the oppressed, and the needy. In this name Elijah challenged King Ahab, "Thus says the Lord, 'You have killed and also taken possession; in the place where dogs lick up the blood of Naboth shall dogs lick your own blood.' " This was the word of the Lord to a king who did not understand justice and mercy and compassion, who robbed his people of their land and then turned around and killed them. In this name Jeremiah said to King Jehoiakim, "Do justice and righteousness, deliver from the hand of the oppressor those who have been wronged. But you, you King Jehoiakim, you have eyes and heart only for dishonest gain, for shedding innocent blood, and for practicing oppression and violence. You shall die and your people shall not cry for you." In this name Ezekiel spoke of judgment to the rulers of Israel:

Shepherds of Israel, you do not feed my sheep, the weak you have not strength-ened, the sick you have not healed, the crippled you have not bound up, the strayed you have not brought back, the lost you have not sought. With falseness and harshness you have ruled over them. Thus says the Lord: behold, I am against those shepherds, and I will rescue my sheep from their bonds. You shall no longer eat my sheep. I will seek the lost, I will bring back the strayed, I will bind up the crippled, I will strengthen the weak, and I will feed them with justice.

This is the name in which prophets have to stand up and speak to the people, but this is also the name in which prophets have to stand up and speak the Word of God to rulers who do not want to listen, who consistently disobey God's laws, who persist in oppression and in vi-olence. This is the name that has become alive in Jesus of Nazareth. This is the name which proclaims sight for the blind, liberty for the captives, and good news for the poor. This name is power and love, justice and mercy.

When we called for a day of prayer to remove unjust structures of oppression in this country and for the removal of those who continue to do injustice to God's people, who continue to live off the suffering and oppression of God's people in this country, there were many people who were upset. There were people who talked about churches that have been divided by this call. The press has used this for its own political ends, and to this day South African television has refused to broadcast the second of the statements of the South African Council of Churches in which the council very clearly said that it affirms the call for this day. I have seen articles in newspapers that I never would have dreamed would be published, secular newspapers that spoke the propaganda of the South African government day by day, that often do not even know how to spell the name Jesus. They have offered to pray for us because we are so misguided.

Yet this has been one of the most affirmative signs that we are right; because they are so desperate, it must be close to the bone. Today we say to them, "We will not take up our guns against you. We will not ask people, as you do, to go out on the streets of the nation and shoot people down like dogs. We will not ask God to bless our guns as you did on December 16 so that you could kill other people and then rob the land." When we made this call we were very clear. I said that day in Johannesburg that we do not believe in the power of violence, but that we believe in the power of prayer. They know this and that is why they are upset, that is why they are angry, that is why they are fearful. They know that the God we worship is a living God, he is a powerful God, he is a God of justice. This God will not turn away from his people, this God will rise up, this God will deliver us from the hands of those evil men who think and do violence to God's defenseless people. I believe that this will *happen.* So when they ask us by which power do you do this, by which name do you do this, we will say, "We do this in the name of this Jesus who taught us what God is like."

The people who have challenged us, the people who have said we are asking for violence, the people who are angry with us; those are the people who do not *know* what it means to suffer because of the color of your skin. They do not *know* what it means to be in jail because you do not have a pass book. They do not *know* what it means to sit under sheets of plastic in Crossroads when the rains of the Cape winter fall. They do not *know* what it means to bury your children who die of hunger in this land where there is so much wealth. They do not *know* what it means to get up in the morning and not know whether by night you will be in jail or back with your family. They do not *know* what it means to live in so-called white South Africa for eleven months of the year and return for three weeks at the end of the year to your homeland, to your family where you are a stranger to your own children. Because they do not know this, because they do not feel this pain, because it is impossible for them to feel our pain, they say to us, "By what name and by what power do you do this, who gave you the right?" We will say as humbly but as clearly as we can, "By the name of Jesus whom you have killed, but whom God has raised up—in his name are we doing this."

Peter's testimony was a theological issue, but at the same time it was a political issue, for he was dragged before the senate, the highest civil authority for the Jewish population at that time. They were the people who had been entrusted with some political power by the Romans. We know this from letters the Romans sent to Jerusalem which always began in this way: "To the government, the senate, and the people of Jerusalem." They were under the system the Romans had devised; they were responsible for law and order and for religion—for all Jewish issues. One could almost say they were responsible for their "own affairs" in Jerusalem. Jesus of Nazareth was executed by the Romans because they regarded him to be a rebel against Caesar. Caesar proclaimed himself lord; he called himself the savior of the people. Jesus of Nazareth came and said, "No, that is not the truth. I *am* the Savior of the people, I *am* Lord, God has made *me* so for the Spirit of the Lord is upon me." Caesar could not understand that; Caesar could not tolerate that, so Jesus in his love and in his mercy and his justice became a threat to the political power of Caesar and by the same token became a threat to the political power of the prophets of Caesar in Jerusalem. You see our struggle did not begin yesterday or in 1960 or in 1910; it is an old, old story.

Now this Jesus, who had been killed because he dared call himself Lord, his name is alive again, and Peter stands up and proclaims, "Therefore let all Israel be assured of this: God has made this Jesus whom you crucified Lord and Christ." This is a political statement, and it becomes, therefore, a political threat. They thought they had disposed of him, but no, here they are confronted by him once again, through the life and the witness of a small, weak, but very clear little church. Yes, the name of Jesus Christ brings healing, the name of Jesus Christ brings power, the name of Jesus Christ brings transformation in the world; but it also brings confrontation with the powers of evil in this world. It is a powerful name, but it is also a vulnerable name; it can be misused and betrayed.

In the name of Jesus, the Christian church so often in our history has forsaken the poor, the weak, and the needy. It has become a church where the poor no longer felt comfort nor any challenge to their own situation. Is it not the fault of our own lives that the church or religion has become the opium of the people; the fault of the church that it is afraid to walk in the footsteps of her Lord who said, "Those who take up the sword shall perish by the sword"? In the name of Jesus the church justified racism and apartheid in this country. Using biblical verses it built a theology around apartheid, defending it on biblical grounds in the name of Jesus. In our country people are despised, in the name of Jesus, because of the color of their skin.

This government says it is a Christian government. We have a new constitution which begins with the proclamation of Christian faith, a constitution which says that it is to uphold Christian standards; yet this Christian constitution deprives us of our human dignity and our human rights. In South Africa families are broken up for the sake of economic gain and exploitation, and starvation wages are being paid. In the eastern Cape I have heard that even today, on farms in the areas around Humansdorp and Jansenville, our people earn six rand a month, ten rand a month, fifteen rand a month. The age of slavery is *not* over. And in this country the people's birthright is being taken away. You wake up one morning and someone has signed a pact with Mr. P. W. Botha, you have a new homeland, and you are no longer a child of this land. In this country the greed of the few guarantees an ongoing poverty for the masses of our people. In this country it is not love and justice but hatred and fear that rules supreme. In this country our people say, "We can no longer stand this; we can no longer take this suffering; we can no longer watch our children die. We will rise up, and we will say that apartheid is wrong." When this happens they are banned like Johnnie Yssel or thrown in jail and tortured to death like Steve Biko and so many others. The strength of our nation are killed, mown down like dogs, as happened on bloody Thursday in Langa and Uitenhage. In the *name* of Jesus this is happening.

In the *name* of Jesus this is happening—in the *name* of Jesus. For as long as the people who rule this country and those who vote for them say that they are Christians, that they base themselves upon the word of God, that their word is a testimony to this Jesus whom we believe in and who died on the cross, the Christian church must rise up and say, "No, it is not true. It is a *lie*. You betray the name of Jesus."

As long as this happens the church must rise up and say, "You can claim what you want but we shall tell you that God says, 'You shall not take my name in vain.' " As long as this happens the church must rise up and say, "You shall reap what you sow." As long as this happens the church must rise up and say, "It is not those who say 'Lord, Lord,' who will enter into the kingdom of heaven, but those who learn to do the will of my Father who is in heaven." No matter how many times you say, "I am a Christian," no matter how many times you read your Bible, no matter how many times you rise up in Parliament and say that we stand under almighty God, God's judgment will come down on you. The church will say it, and I will say it today, not because I am better, not because I think I am stronger, not because we have power, but because it is God's own truth. And if the church is afraid to speak God's truth then we might as well throw this Bible in the sea. So in the name of Jesus, the name of Jesus is being betrayed.

But the name of Jesus can never be used to justify exploitation, it can never be used to justify the wanton killing of our people, it can never be used to justify oppression and suffering. It is a name of power, it is a name of liberation, it is a name of love, it is a name of compassion, it is a name of justice, it is a name of peace. Those who know the name of Jesus know peace; those who know the name of Jesus know justice, and they will stand up and fight. In this name we stand, in this name we pray for justice and for peace, in this name we pray for the crumbling of unjust structures. I think that they are shouting so loudly out there because they do not want us to hear already the crumbling of the walls. In this name we shall have faith; in this name we shall continue to pray and continue to make ourselves available to God.

To pray does not mean that I will now fold my hands and close my eyes and sit back and let God do all the work. To pray means that I will say to God, "I am now at your disposal. *Use* me: use me for *peace,* use me for *justice,* use me for *compassion,* use me for *mercy,* use me for *love,* use me for *liberation* so that your people can see." I believe that God will hear us as we pray for the removal of those who persist in disobeying God's will. I believe that God has *seen* us. I believe that God will *hear* us. I believe that God will *use* us.

And so my brothers and sisters gathered for this prayer service today, let us look upon the name of Jesus which spells peace and love, mercy and justice, compassion and freedom. Let us stand in the name of Jesus. Let us believe that this land will one day be a land where we can live in peace with one another. Let us believe that this land will become a land where we will no longer be looked down upon because of the color of our skin. Let us believe that this land will become a land where there is security for our children and that it will lie in our love and our search for justice and not in guns and tanks and police forces. This land will become a land in which we shall be able to build up God's kingdom and all that is part of that kingdom. Because we believe this, we shall stand, we shall be clear, we shall be counted, we shall speak so that they can hear from Cape Town to Pretoria, from Port Elizabeth to Durban, from any little hovel in this country to the highest councils of authority. "Our Father," we will say, "who art in heaven, give us, all our people, our daily bread so that we will not die of hunger. And forgive us our sins, even that sin of being afraid to stand up and be counted for justice, and we will forgive those that trespass against us. And lead us not into temptation, but deliver us from evil. For *thine* is the kingdom, for *thine* is the power, for *thine* is the glory for ever and ever. Amen."

11

If South Africa Had Listened

I want today to try to understand what it means that we in this country have a document called the Freedom Charter. It is a document that we can be rightly proud of. Indeed, it is a document that represents, better than any other document ever written in this country, the political aspirations of our people. It represents the dream of South Africa's people. It represents what it is that we want. It represents what we long for. It represents the expression of our desires about what kind of country we want. No other document, whether it was thought up by the British government, or whether it was drafted by the Nationalist government, or whether it was drafted by any other political party in this country, has ever been able so to capture the imagination of our people and so to inspire us in the struggle for justice, for freedom, and for liberation.

Today, June 26, 1985, it has been exactly thirty years since the people of this country, black and white together, came to Kliptown to formulate what has become known as the Freedom Charter. The Freedom Charter is the most democratic document that we know.

In this document we hope, and I hope, that our young people of today will find the necessary inspiration to continue to work and fight for a South Africa which one day will reflect the desires that live in the hearts of our people.

Let me remind you, my brothers and sisters, of the preamble to the Freedom Charter. It is so beautiful. Listen to these words:

We the people of South Africa declare for all our country and all the world to know:

—that South Africa belongs to all who live in it, black and white, and that no government can justly claim authority, unless it is based on the will of the people.

On June 26, 1955, a coalition of South Africans opposed to apartheid signed a document called the Freedom Charter. This speech was given on the thirtieth anniversary of that event, June 26, 1985.

—that our people have been robbed of their birthright to land, liberty and peace by a form of government founded on injustice and inequality.

—that our country will never be prosperous or free until all our people live in brotherhood, enjoying equal rights and opportunities.

—that only a democratic state, based on the will of the people can secure to all our people, the birthright without distinction of color, race, sex, or belief.

and therefore, we the people of South Africa, black and white together, equals, countrymen and brothers, adopt this Freedom Charter, and we pledge ourselves to strive together sparing nothing of our strength and our courage, until the democratic changes here set out, have been won.

These are the words that have become a foundation upon which we have built our struggle. These are the words that have grown to cosmic proportions; these are the words that eclipse even now the roar of the guns and the troop carriers in our townships. Even above the clatter of the violence of the South African government, even above the cries of violence and fear that emanate from those people who want to maintain oppression in South Africa, we hear the sound of the Freedom Charter. Even above the laws that they make that they try to force down our throats, we hear the words of the Freedom Charter. And even above the speeches that are being made by the state president and all those people he has put in power, even to those stooges in the colored parliament, we hear the words of the Freedom Charter. And while these words, my brothers and sisters, inspire us, and while these words make us rise to every occasion, and while these words spell out for us the path that we have dedicated ourselves to walk without fear, and with clarity of mind, while we have this, we understand. So let the people of Britain and the United States see how the young people of South Africa come together to talk about this important document.

While we are here tonight let us think about what that means. My brothers and sisters, it was young people who came together at the time that the Freedom Charter was adopted, at the time that our people, your fathers and mothers, those who have gone before us in the struggle, those who have said, even then, that we shall not give up until the day arrives that we and our children shall be free. When they came together the dismal record of this country, of oppression and dispossession and disenfranchisement, was already very, very clear. It was three hundred years old by then. They were living then under the constitution of 1910, a constitution which left no room for black people in this country to participate in the government, no room for black people in this country to help to shape the future of the land of their birth, no room for us to make our own contribution to make this country great. It was a constitution that excluded the majority of the people. They lived under a constitution that left room for further disenfranchisement, a constitution that left room for unjust structures and for bantustan policies.

By then also, we must not forget, apartheid was eight years old. By then they could already feel the damage that this system was doing to this country and to our people, and they could already begin to anticipate the damage that would be done to our people by this system later. Already then, even when apartheid was only eight years old, they could see the irreparable damage done to race relations. Even then it was clear that the draconian laws that had been put on the statute books, laws like the Suppression of Communism Act, would not disappear, but would multiply. Even then they could see how this country would be shaped, not by hope, not by justice, and not by truth, but by lies and by despair and by the desperation of evil men who only knew the language of violence and threat and intimidation and racism. Even then, even when apartheid was only eight years old, others were already shaping what was to become known as the theology of apartheid. Even then, others were looking for arguments in the Bible that they could use to justify their oppression so that they could continue to say God is on our side. Even then, others were beginning to shape the lie that would become the core of the propaganda of the South African government.

Then, even as now, as our people came together to say no to this growing menace to our humanity, to say no to this monster that was being created by the people of this country who had the vote and who kept that government in power; even then as our people came together to seek a new future, to seek a new direction, to ask different questions, and to say, "We do not want this for ourselves; we do not want this for our children; we want a different land; we want another kind of future"—even then the meetings were broken up by police, as our meetings are today. Even then, our people were intimidated, as we are being intimidated today. I hear that first we had this hall we are meeting in tonight, then we were told we could not have the hall, then we were told again, yes, we can have the hall, and then we were told, no, we couldn't. And then the security police came here and tried to intimidate the people who said we could use the hall so that they would withdraw their permission. Ha! What do they think of our people? Do they think that we will really run away and say, "Oh yes, Baas. . . ." Don't they know that those days are over? Don't they know those days are long gone?

Even back then, they did what they do today. Even then, our people's homes were raided as our homes are raided today. Even then, our people were detained, kept without trial, never charged. Even then, our people were tortured in their jails as our people are tortured and murdered now. Even then, our leaders were banned and could not speak to us as our people today face treason charges and are kept in jail and not allowed to stand up and speak the truth that comes from the heart of South Africa's oppressed and suffering people. Even then, the government was as afraid of that truth as they are now. Even then, they were as fearful of us as they are now—not because we hate them, not because we are going to kill them, but because they know injustice never pays. The day shall come when they shall hear our words come true, because they know it is true: "You shall reap what you sow." That's why they are afraid.

So the charter, my brothers and sisters, came not out of the minds of people who sat behind desks and simply thought academically about the issue. The charter does not come out of a classroom situation. The Freedom Charter was not born in a discussion among academics. The Freedom Charter was born in the hearts of the people of this country who are oppressed. The Freedom Charter came out of our lives. The Freedom Charter is the child of our suffering, the child of our oppression; it is the child also of our hope and the child of our expectation of a better future for this country. The Freedom Charter could never have been born in a Nationalist government. The Freedom Charter could only have been born in the hearts of those who understand hypocrisy, who love freedom, and who seek justice.

And so, my brothers and sisters, the moment the Freedom Charter was adopted, the South African government said, "Communism! subversion! treason!" We learned then that it was subversive to say: "South Africa belongs to all its people." We learned then that it is treason to say: "Freedom in our lifetime." We learned then that it is treason to say: "Freedom for all." We learned then that it is treason to say to our

people: "Let us rise up and let us act together so that we can establish
freedom and humanity and decency in our land." The people who said
that then were hauled before the courts of this land or thrown in jail or
put in Robben Island, and some of them are still there—like Nelson
Mandela.

But we have also learned some other things. We have learned that
the same government who called our people communists and atheists
because we believe in freedom, and the same people who therefore
imply that we are not Christian, that we do not understand the Bible,
that we do not know the name of Jesus—they are the people who betray
the name of Jesus. They betrayed the name of Jesus, for in the name
of this Jesus—which is a name, in case you don't know, that spells
liberation and freedom and humanity and justice and wholeness and
reconciliation and peace—in this name, they have created apartheid.
In this name they break up black family life. In this name, for economic
gain and for the sake of exploitation, they create pass laws and influx
control laws, and they separate men from their families, bring them
into South Africa, and keep them here for eleven months of the year
so they can go back to their children and to their wives only at the end
of the year for a measly three weeks after they have become strangers
to their own children. In the name of Jesus they did this. In the name
of Jesus they stole our land, and they made us strangers in the land of
our birth. In this name they pay starvation wages so that our people will
remain poor. Our people are not poor because South Africa is poor.
Our people are not poor because we do not want to work. Our people
are poor because the rich are so rich, and our people are poor because
we are consistently exploited and because we are consistently kept poor
by a system that needs us to be poor.

In the name of Jesus these people have created bantustans, those
concentration camps the South African government euphemistically
calls relocation areas, where our old people die of despair and hopelessness and where our children die of hunger and malnutrition. They
have done this. In the name of Jesus they sent their army into our
townships; they sent their police into our townships; they shoot our
people as if we were dogs. And in the name of Jesus they turn around
and say, like the Kannemeyer Commission, that the police are not to
blame. The South African government must know and they must understand. You cannot take the name of the Lord your God in vain. And

one day they shall pay for what they are doing to God's defenseless
people in this country. They must understand that.

The same government that despises the Freedom Charter are the
people who have systematically taken away whatever constitutional rights
we have had. They are the people who then turned around and gave us
dummy institutions like "Colored Management Committees" and "Urban Bantu Councils" and an "Indian House of Delegates." Far from
living up to their proclaimed democracy, they don't know the meaning
of the word. The people who despise the Freedom Charter and who
say the Freedom Charter is a document not suitable for South Africa
are the ones who reject our participation and our contribution to this
society. And they then create a new constitution, which is again built
upon racism and which again entrenches apartheid and white minority
rule, and they turn around and say to us: "You must go for this; you
can participate; this is now a democracy." They must be joking.

And yet, we must ask the question, my brothers and sisters, why
are they so afraid of the Freedom Charter? Why are they so afraid of
the ideals of the Freedom Charter? They are people who look at the
Freedom Charter and say: "This is not a good document: it is too vague,
it is not radical enough, it is muddled thinking, it is not clear enough."
But why then are they so afraid of it? Why can't we celebrate the
Freedom Charter without interference? Why can't we talk about the
charter and why can't the charter become the basis for a new society
in South Africa?

I will tell you why. They say that the things enshrined in the Freedom
Charter are treason and subversion because it says that the people shall
govern. The people shall govern—not some little group of white people
who think that because they are white they have the right to govern
everybody else. Not some little group of people who have been made
honorary whites and can therefore sit in those "little houses" next to
parliament and then say that they are parliament. But the people shall
govern. Not the elite, not the rich, not the wealthy, not the clever, but
the people shall govern—you will govern. That's why they are so afraid.
Not the army shall govern, not the police shall govern, not P. W. Botha
shall govern—you shall govern.

You see what the Freedom Charter talks about is rights for everybody. The Freedom Charter says that all land shall be shared, it shall
not belong to one little group, and it shall never again be divided on
the 13 percent or whatever else percent basis. And there shall never be

talk about white South Africa and bantustans anymore. The Freedom Charter says the doors of learning shall be open to all. No bantu education anymore, no "kleurling" education anymore, no Indian education anymore, no "Boere" education anymore. The Freedom Charter says there shall be houses for all our people, there shall be decent shelter for all our people, but not while some people live in castles and in palaces while the masses of our people have to live in these shanties that they built in our townships so they can come around and say, "Oh, aren't you lucky because look: you have a house."

That is what the charter says, and that is why they are so afraid. Because if these demands are met, then we will all be equal. And then if you go into a job you will be judged on your ability to work and not on the color of your skin. Why are they afraid when we say that there shall be peace and there shall be friendship? The question we must ask is: "Why is it a crime in South Africa to say there shall be peace and there shall be friendship?" Because if you say there shall be peace, there can be no more apartheid. If you say there shall be peace, the army should not be in the townships. If you say there shall be peace, the police should not come out and kill our children. If you say there shall be peace, we will all be equal before the law. If you say there shall be peace, we shall be paid for our work. If you say there shall be peace, those people who are in parliament now will not be in parliament. That is what it means. If you say there shall be peace and equality and that the society is open, then Mr. Louis Le Grange will have to accept my challenge to debate him on television.

But all of this is treason; it is dangerous for the South African government because it is a government that is not a government of the people. It is a government based on injustice and oppression. It is a government that is not democratic, and the people in it are not representative; they are illegitimate, and therefore they ought not to be where they are.

That is why we came together on Sunday, June 16, and we prayed to God: "Remove these people who are so unjust and who persist in disobeying your will." And then they get angry and then they get upset—even the church leaders get upset. Why do they get upset? Do you know what they do? On every December 16 they get together and pray that God will bless their guns so that they can kill other people and steal their land. They pray for that. We do not pray for that. All we said was: "God, you see us. You see our oppression, you see our suffering, you see what we are going through, and you know who is responsible for this. It is not the devil, unless the devil lives in Pretoria now." And so we have said to God: "Just take them away." I did not pray for the state president's death; I simply prayed to God to give him another job—to send him into retirement.

Why are they afraid? First of all they say that you cannot prescribe to God, because God will not listen to you then. And they know. But even with all their lies, even with all their untruthfulness, even with all their hypocrisy, they know that basically the truth is there. The God to whom we are praying is a God of justice, a God of liberation, and a God of freedom. He will come down, and he will deliver his people from the hand of the Pharaoh—whether he lives in Egypt or whether he lives in Groote Schuur or whether he lives in Pretoria. It will happen. And we know that they are therefore singing their last song. The time of this government is over. They are in their last death throe, and that is why they are doing what they are doing.

You know why they pay those ministers so very much money? They know that they are not going to be there for very long. And so what we are talking about is that we know that our struggle will not be in vain. What we are talking about is that we know that our struggle is just. What we are talking about is that we know that our people are not dying in vain. What we are talking about is that we know our children's blood is not being spilled in vain. What we are talking about is that we know that we have not struggled for all these years simply to sit in a hall and sing. We have struggled to be free; we have struggled so that the ideals enshrined in this Freedom Charter will become a reality.

And so, my brothers and sisters, I want to appeal to the people of this land even at this late hour to accept the demands and the ideals and the dream of the Freedom Charter. For the Freedom Charter in its very essence is the voice of the people of South Africa. If South Africa had only listened then in 1955, there would have been a democracy in this country. If South Africa had only listened then in 1955, detention without trial would have disappeared. Our people would never have been tortured in their jails, and Steve Biko and Reddy Sela and all the others would not have died at the hands of the police while they were in jail. If South Africa had listened, there would have been no home-lands. If South Africa had listened to the voice of its people in 1955, apartheid would have died long before it had become the monster that it is today.

If South Africa had only listened, there would have been far less violence in this country. The government would not have to depend on the army and the police and upon military violence to maintain its power, but the government would have had the love and the respect and the loyalty and the support of all its people.

If South Africa had only listened. If South Africa had only listened, Sharpeville would not have happened. If South Africa had listened to the voice of the people in the Freedom Charter, our children would not have died on the streets of Soweto in 1976. If South Africa had only listened, our people from Kwanobuhle and Langa would not have been killed here in Uitenhage. If South Africa had only listened, the massacre of bloody Thursday would not have occurred. If South Africa had only listened to the voice of the people then, we would have had a better future.

And yet they have decided to ignore the voice of our people. So, my people, listen to me tonight. Take the Freedom Charter and the demands and the dream of the Freedom Charter once again and make them your own. Base your future upon these basic foundations. It is not a faultless document, but it does enshrine the best that any country can offer its people in the world today. It is the only meaningful alternative to this evil system under which we must suffer so today. Therefore take these ideals. Make them your own. Take this dream and make it your own. Take this aspiration of our people in the Freedom Charter and make it your own. Take the ideals of the Freedom Charter and make them your own.

We do not need to become like the oppressor. The Freedom Charter has spelled out what the people of South Africa want to be. They do not need to become slaves of the violence of apartheid. The Freedom Charter has spelled out a better way. We do not need to remain slaves of a racist society. The Freedom Charter has spelled out a better way. We do not need to remain the slaves of capitalist exploitation. The Freedom Charter has spelled out a better way.

And so let us come together. Let us seek the liberty that our people sought in 1955, and let us make that once again a unity in 1985. Let us move forward knowing that the words of the charter are the dream of our people. And let us say together tonight, for ourselves and for our children, that these are freedoms we will fight for side by side throughout our lives until we have won our liberty. God bless you!

12

Raise a Sign of Hope

My brothers and sisters, I am grateful that I can be with you today. I have come to Cradock often in the past years. The first time was when Matthew Goniwe and Fort Calata were detained, and the people of Cradock asked me to come and visit with them, to come and see for myself what was happening in Lingilihle.

Since then I have learned to admire those men who have been such wonderful leaders in this community, and it has been a singular honor for me to work with them over the last year. I will not forget the last time I spoke in this very town of Cradock some five or six weeks ago. The people who came to listen were willing to wait from eight o'clock in the evening until I arrived at almost eleven o'clock. They did not move, which was a sign of the spirit that lived in Cradock. And that was a tribute to the leadership of the brothers whom we mourn today, and whom we will bury. When I think of their lives, when I think of what they have become—a symbol of our struggle, of our hope, of our determination, of our genius that we have in the black community in South Africa—and I think that we must bury them today, I must say so that all the world and this country can hear: if we have to bury men like Matthew Goniwe, men like our brothers Calata, Mkhonto, and Mhlawuli, then I say this country is digging its own grave. South Africa is setting fire to its own future.

As I stand here today I am overcome by a terrible sadness and an anger, and I know that this sadness hangs all over our land. Because yet again, as so many times this year, we must mourn. Yet again we must bury our people. Yet again we must come and lay to rest some of the finest sons and daughters of our country. Yet again this government has shown that it will be utterly ruthless in its determination to hold on to power and to keep apartheid alive. Yet again we must say that something terrible is happening to this country. Look at where we are! Look

---

This is a funeral address delivered in Cradock on July 20, 1985 at the burial of Matthew Goniwe, Fort Calata, Sicelo Mhlawuli, and Thomas Mkhonto, victims of the violence of that summer.

at where we are! Apartheid with its racism and its exploitation is not only alive but is being defended with uncommon harshness. The church is being persecuted for its obedience to God and for its decision to stand alongside the poor and the weak and the oppressed of our country.

There is unrest all over South Africa, for the cause of all the unrest and the violence has not yet been removed. The police and the army have laid siege to our townships. As our brother has said, indeed "our townships are infested with them." The police and the army are conducting a reign of terror over our people. Our people disappear; we do not know what happens to them. Over the past few months more than ten thousand people have been detained and kept in jail. Thousands have been wounded, hundreds have been killed. Over the past few months there has been the emergence of death squads. I am not so sure that they are simply death squads put there by the so-called right-wing, for they have received too much protection over the last year. Our children die, like little Johannes Pochter the other day in Steytlerville, only twelve years old, beaten to death by the police. Our children die like they have been dying for so many years now in those concentration camps in the resettlement areas where there is no food and where there will be no nourishment from the moment they are born until the very week that they die, which will not be long after that.

This says to me that we must face up to the fact, my brothers and sisters, that in this government we are facing truly the spiritual children of Adolf Hitler. This is where we are. And today we are burying our brothers—who have not died by accident, nor is their death a mystery to us.

Our people who live here in the townships have testified, and they know what the truth is about these people and about the deaths of our brothers. Therefore we do not share those newspaper reports which talk about the mystery of the death of the four that we will bury today. The UDF has raised certain issues and has asked certain fundamental questions about the deaths of Matthew Goniwe and Fort Calata and the other brothers. We have said publicly that only a very few people have known about the meeting that they were attending in Port Elizabeth and that there was no public announcement as to when they would leave that night or whether they would come back to Cradock that evening. Only the people in the office knew that they were going to go back to Cradock that night, and the only other people who could have known were people who could listen in to that conversation with their sophisticated instruments. We know who they are.

We have been told that Matthew had said that evening that he would not stop the car unless he was stopped by uniformed police. We know that there was a roadblock that night. The question that must therefore be answered is: Who killed them? They were not struck down by lightning, the car did not mysteriously go up in flames. Our brothers were killed by the people who stopped them. Our people believe that the police did it—and I believe it too! It is time that we must say to this government: "Stop protecting these murderers who kill our people!" Who has been responsible for the systematic death of a number of our civic leaders over the past year, for they die mysteriously, they disappear mysteriously, they are being assassinated one after the other? Who is responsible for that?

And I want to say to the South African government, "Do *not* protect those people! Why have you created a climate in this country in which our children can be shot down in the streets by a policeman and that policeman can get away with it? Why have you created a climate in which death squads roam around and can do whatever they like as if the lives of our people do not matter? Why have you created a climate in which people know they can kill our leaders and they will not be brought to justice? Why have you created a climate in which the police can kill forty-three of our people without any provocation, and you set up a commission of inquiry, and still the police will be held blameless?" I must say to the South African government, "We have said to you before and we are saying to you again: there is a God in heaven who knows about justice, and you shall reap what you sow!"

And yet, my brothers and sisters, while this is happening, it seems that most of our white brothers and sisters in this country cannot be bothered. They are more concerned about the cancellation of a rugby tour than they are about the lives of our people! I have seen more concern in our newspapers for the "All Blacks" who are not coming to South Africa than for our people who have died. In most of white South Africa, they are calling for stronger tactics by the government. Most refuse to hear the truth, most refuse to listen to the voice of the oppressed and of our people who suffer. They would rather listen to the propaganda on South African television than they would to the voice of Mrs. Goniwe, who will tell them about her husband and what he did and the work he had done for the sake not only of our people but for all of South Africa. While we are suffering, and while we are crying out, white South Africa mostly wants to make heroes out of those black people who are willing to sell their souls for money and the little bit of political power that P. W. Botha will give them.

I must say to our white brothers and sisters, I am so grateful that some of you are here today to show your solidarity. I hope that you will go away from this funeral today with more than merely sympathy in your hearts, because we do not need that. We need your total commitment to the struggle; we need your joining in the struggle; we need your voices to be heard; we need your bodies in the struggle. And so we hope that you will go and use the power that you have, so you can go and tell the government tomorrow that this evil system must be eradicated. You can go and you can tell the government tomorrow that they must stop killing our people. I hope that you will use the opportunities you have to do just that and thereby forge links of brotherhood and sisterhood that cannot be broken even by the evil of racism or by the propaganda of the South African government.

I would plead with white South Africa, please do not be deceived by what you hear and see and by those who so cunningly can twist the truth even by quoting the Bible. The state president spoke a week ago to hundreds of young white people. He said to them that it is his duty to stop terrorism just as Jesus drove out the money changers from the temple. I would like to ask the state president whether he knows what he is doing when he tries to read a theology of violence into the life of the man whom the Bible calls the Prince of Peace. I would like to know why those church leaders who are so quick to condemn us when we ask to pray for the removal of unjust rule and who say that we want violence—why don't they rise up and tell the state president: "You cannot use the name of Jesus to justify your violence." Why are they silent? It is their duty to preach not only to those people who are voiceless but it is even more their duty to preach to those who have the power to change this country tomorrow if they want to.

I would like to say another thing. The state president must think about whether he is right in simply assuming that the terrorists he is talking about are those brothers who have to fight from across the border. The experience of black people in this country is different. We do not think that the terrorists are those who are the freedom fighters of this land. The ANC, Mr. Botha, did not shoot our people when they were defenseless at Sharpeville twenty-five years ago. The ANC, Mr.

Botha, did not kill our children in 1976 when they were walking peacefully on the streets of Soweto. The ANC, Mr. Botha, did not kill our children during the school boycotts in 1980 in Cape Town. It was not the ANC who killed little Thabo Sibeko, who was six years old, last year on the East Rand. It was not the ANC who killed forty-three people at Langa township on March 21 at the massacre of Uitenhage. It was not the ANC who killed our four brothers whom we are burying today. Your government did it—and so *they* are the terrorists! It is a most dangerous thing when people in power begin to believe their own propaganda!

And I urge those white people who are serious about the future of South Africa to look a little further than your newspapers, to listen a little deeper than to the voices of the commentators on South African television, and to come and talk to our people in the townships. There you will hear the truth. There you will see the truth. There you will see what it means to live under apartheid. I know that today's funeral will not be the last one. I know that our mourning will not end today. I know that tomorrow and tomorrow and tomorrow and tomorrow there will be more tears that will flow. And there are difficult days ahead. The violence of the South African government knows no end. More of our brothers and sisters will be detained. There will be more whose names will be added to some hit list, and more will be killed by those faceless murderers who hide behind balaclavas and who hide behind their guns and who hide behind the protection that they get.

But this is the price that we have to pay for our freedom. We are here today, but we will do more than just mourn. We have heard it over and over again. We will not simply mourn; we will wake up from mourning, and we will dedicate ourselves anew to the struggle for justice and liberation and freedom and peace.

If I die tomorrow, do not come to my funeral and sing freedom songs if you are not willing to participate today in the struggle for liberation and justice. If I die tomorrow, do not revenge my death with more senseless violence and hatred, but raise up a sign of hope that this country will become what it must become and that we will make our contribution to that. If I die tomorrow, do not give up and do not despair, for I know that our victory is near and that apartheid and injustice will never endure and that our people shall be free. If I die tomorrow, raise up a sign that the victory of this country is not written in the guns and the violence, and the armies of the South African government, but that the victory and the future of this country are written in the hearts of our people in our determination to be free and in our willingness to give our lives for the struggle that we believe in.

I know that as we have to go from funeral to funeral many of us will become tired. Many of us will become tired of protest, will become tired of knocking at the door, will become tired of seeing our brothers and sisters dying so much. But as long as our people, black and white, are shackled in the chains of oppression and racism, there will be a fight to fight, and we must not give up. As long as our children die needlessly and untimely there will be a fight to fight—do not give up. And as long as injustice still reigns supreme in this land there will be a fight to fight—do not give up. As long as little children are born just to die, too soon, there will be a fight to fight—do not give up. For this country is yours, this land is yours, the future is yours—do not give it up.

So while we mourn, let us commit ourselves again to the struggle for justice and freedom and liberation. There are things that we can do. We can begin to ask ourselves what those of us who come from Natal, and those of us who come from the Western Cape, and those of us who come from Transvaal, should ask ourselves: why it is that the people in the Eastern Cape can have a successful consumer boycott, but we do not do anything about that in the Cape or Natal or Transvaal! One of the things that should come out of this funeral is for the people of this country to go back home and organize for that, and we will lay low those who think they are the powerful. We will keep away from them our buying power. We should begin to do that. We must do it in Cape Town, we must do it in Johannesburg, and we must do it in Durban.

And to our people in the townships who have shops, I say you are part of this struggle too. When we say that we shall boycott the white shops we want your full cooperation. We want you to make it possible for our people to do that. You do not raise your prices, you lower them. You lower them because it is the cause of the struggle. And if you do that you shall be known as people who fight with us and who struggle with us for justice.

I must say that if the only thing we do when we go back home is to raise a sign of hope for our people so that we can see and the world can see that in spite of what is happening to us we are not a defeated people, we will have achieved a noble purpose.

13

If You Believe

My brothers and sisters, I came upon this text today exactly a week ago, while I was in my cell in Pretoria Central Prison, after one of the most difficult weekends in all my life. The first two weeks I could bear. Even the silence, even not being able to speak with anyone, not being able to open my heart, not being able to share my feelings, my fears, my anxieties, or my longings. Not being able to tell anyone how much I missed my wife and my children, my family, my congregation. It was only in those days that I discovered how much I love this congregation in Bellville and how much all of you have become part of my heart and of my life and why it is that God, through very difficult days—and you know those days—has kept me in this congregation for nine years now.

But the third week became almost too much for me. By 3 o'clock in the afternoon they bring your supper. By 3:30 they lock up and slam the grill in your cell and double-lock it. They slam the steel door and double-lock that too, and finally the two grills in the passage. That Friday afternoon of the third week was no different. As I sat silently in my cell, the noises of the wardens leaving the prison building faded away and on the floor above me I could hear the other prisoners talking with one another, reading the newspapers of the day, discussing, sometimes laughing—and I had no one to share this with. No one to talk to.

I had been on my knees almost constantly for three weeks, praying to God to lead me out of that darkness and out of that pain and out of that suffering. And nothing happened. Then the moment came when I fell on my knees and I cried as I never cried before. Maybe for the first time since I was a little boy. I then said to God, "I do not understand this. Why have you brought me here? It's been three weeks now, God, and I have prayed every day and I have tried to believe that you in your power will take me out of this place of imprisonment and bring

---

This was the first sermon preached by Allan Boesak after his release from three weeks of solitary confinement. He delivered it to his own Bellville congregation on September 22, 1985.

me out into the world again, to the community of the living again." For when you are locked up like that you sometimes feel as good as dead.

For three weeks I have believed that somehow God would work through the international community to put pressure on the South African government to let me out. After three weeks, that did not happen. All my life I have tried to hold onto my faith. I have preached the gospel as honestly as I could because I believe that Jesus has called me to do that. I said to God, "Why, if I am your servant, if I have tried to do what is right in this world, have you done this to me? I have said it all. You know, God, what happened to me in this year, in 1985. Wasn't that enough? Why must I now sit here in this prison, not understanding, not seeing any way out of this?" I wrestled with God. I fought with God. I said to him, "I was a fool! If I were a little more clever, I would have accepted those positions that were offered me in America, to become a professor of theology at a world-renowned university. I could have pursued the nomination to become the General Secretary of the World Council of Churches. I could at least have asked my supporters, yes, please lobby for me. Instead, I wrote to the search committee and said no, I do not want this position because I believe that my place, at this time in history, is in South Africa. If I were wise, I could have taken my wife and my children and left South Africa, because I know what happens to people in this land who try to struggle for justice and for peace. If I had done this," I said to God, "my wife and my children would have been with me. If I had done this, I would have been safe now. If I had done this, I would not have been in this place now." I said to God, "You made me believe that the struggle for justice and human dignity, the struggle for peace and humanity in South Africa is also *your* struggle. You made me believe, from the very beginning, that my opposition to the South African government was never of my own. It was an opposition that was based always upon my faith in Jesus Christ and upon the certain knowledge that apartheid is a heresy and that it cannot be defended on the basis of the gospel. I believed that my involvement in the political struggle for the sake of the weak and the poor and the needy is an integral part of my discipleship, is the heart of my discipleship in this country. This is what you, God, have called me to do. Why have you made me believe this and yet brought me to this place?"

I do not mind telling you this morning, my brothers and sisters, that that was the most difficult moment of my life. As I was there on my knees, the words couldn't come anymore and there were no more tears to cry. Friday night went by and Saturday morning dawned and there was still no answer. Saturday night came, and I wrestled through the night and still I found no answer. My difficulty with this God whom we cannot see, whom we have to believe in although he will not break through the prison walls and make his voice plain to me so that I could hear another voice apart from my own to reassure me, became unbearable. I thought to myself: I have always preached from this pulpit (and you are my witnesses!) that I believe in the power of God. That Jesus Christ is Lord and King and that therefore no government on earth can detain the power of God. But as I sat there in that jail and as the days and the nights crawled by and that weekend dawned upon me and I still could see only darkness, I said to myself, "Am I to believe that the power of P. W. Botha and Louis Le Grange is greater than the power of this almighty God?"

But on Sunday morning I opened my Bible to read. I am not one of those who believe that you just open the Bible and mysteriously God will show you a passage. But I opened my Bible to find a word of consolation, a word of light, a word of inspiration, a word of truth that would take away from me my uncertainty, my fear, my anxiety—a word that I could hold on to. And without my having looked for it, my Bible fell open at the Gospel of Mark, chapter 9, and like the blast of a trumpet the words of Jesus fell on my ears: "If you believe, all things are possible to those who believe." And then I knew. That night, Sunday, September 15, I sat down and wrote a letter to my wife and said to her: "I have wrestled with God and it is over. I now know that I will be with you before the weekend."

In this passage I saw my own dilemma as I came to understand the dilemma of this father who brought his sick child to Jesus. The dilemma of this father begins with the fact that his child was ill. Today we would say that this child was an epileptic. All the symptoms were there. But in those days they did not know this. They only saw something they did not understand, that threatened their existence, their lives, and the meaning and worth of their lives. And when they experienced something that threatened the good order of God as God meant it to be, the only way they could express their feelings of fear was to say: "This is an evil spirit." They understood their struggle as not so much against the illness, but as a struggle against the spirit of evil that had seized this boy, that had this boy in its grip, that would not let go, that would kill this boy. "Sometimes," the father said to Jesus, "the spirit will grab him and throw him in the water, and sometimes in the fire." He might burn to death any moment; he might drown any moment. What was he to do?

The issue here is not merely their inadequate understanding or our knowledge of illness based on modern scientific methods and research. Neither is it a question of our superiority, since we no longer speak of "evil spirits" when someone is ill. There is something more to this. We like to believe that through our scientific know-how we have conquered all. We make believe that we can control everything—including life and death. We have conquered the world and we have enslaved nature. We colonize the heavens, and we plant our silly little flags and nationalistic symbols on the planets and the stars. We take giant steps for humankind, or so we claim, and we wait for God to crawl back into his corner and leave the world to be run by those who through their knowledge and power can do it—namely us. But we cannot face the reality of evil, neither in our world nor in ourselves. Yes, we conquer space and we win battles against killer germs. Yet at the same time we are destroying the world and we *create* killer germs and nuclear arms, enough to destroy not only *this* world but also worlds yet undiscovered. We want to create life while we still have not learned to respect life. The same governments who claim to be the protectors of the unborn child dish out medals of honor to the soldier who kills more efficiently than the "enemy." But we ignore or deny these contradictions because we do not want to face the reality of evil.

The gospel wants to tell us very clearly that evil is real. Let us make no mistake. Evil in this world is real, it is tangible; you can see it, you can taste it, you can feel it, you can experience it. For anything, anything at all that goes against the will of God, anything that threatens our human existence, anything that destroys humanity, anything that is violent, or destructive, or inhuman, is evil, and that evil is real. That is something we so-called modern people have lost sight of. So we have no reason to say, "Oh, in those times they were primitive. They did not understand as we understand; it is out of ignorance that they spoke of evil spirits." No, people of God, no, even today we must understand that evil is real. And evil spirits in this world are real. Let me say again: anything that goes against the will of God for this world, that tries to destroy the vision that God has for this world—of peace and justice, of human dignity and wholeness, of life and love of the community—

that is evil and it is real. That is why it makes sense that the Apostle Paul writes:

For we are not contending against flesh and blood, but against the principalities, against the powers, against the world rulers of this present darkness, against the spiritual hosts of wickedness in the heavenly places. (Eph. 6:12)

This is true. When we confront the utter callousness of people who will do anything at all, destroy anyone at all, simply to hold on to power, then you must understand that evil is real. We are facing a government that will allow children to die of hunger, that will allow people to be shot on the street as if their lives do not matter. When this happens, you must know that evil is real. And when lawlessness dresses up as law and when inhumanity and brutality pose as law and order, when injustice claims to be justice and when the heresy of apartheid is defended as Christian, evil is real. Christian churches send telegrams when we plan peaceful protests against this government, because our resistance threatens their vested interests. But when we are thrown in jail under a law that should not even have existed, that is a travesty of justice, a denial of every basic human right, they keep quiet. When our people are terrorized, when the police and the army make war against our defenseless children, when pregnant women and our old people are beaten with sjamboks and brutally assaulted in their own homes, they are quiet. When our young people are shot to death for daring to resist, they do not speak or send telegrams of protest. No, they are as quiet as the graves our children lie in. When this happens, evil is real.

And let us not say that evil spirits existed only in the times of Jesus when people were "primitive." No, my brothers and sisters, evil exists in this country, even now. Evil dresses itself up in black ties and black suits and top hats, and sits in parliament and makes the laws that undermine the dignity of the people of South Africa. Evil sits in parliament and defends the cold-blooded murder of our leaders. Evil stands on the pulpit and justifies the oppression and on-going violence of apartheid. Evil sits in padded chairs in air-conditioned boardrooms, continues the financing of apartheid, and self-righteously claims it is protecting the poor. And in the meantime the prophets of God are silenced, not because we want to kill or destroy or hate, but because we preach a message of peace, love, and justice. We are thrown in jail because that message of truth is too much to bear for those who live on untruths.

Let me make it clear to you. Even today, I have not given up my conviction for our nonviolent struggle for justice in this country. If it is God's will, it is God's struggle—and I will continue to do that for as long as God gives me breath in my body. I want to say to my people: Do not give up this struggle. We must not turn to violence, because violence will destroy us as much as it has destroyed the people who are using it against us. Violence will destroy our soul even as their violence has destroyed their souls. They have no wisdom left, they have no understanding, they have no insight. They have no God left except the god of their guns, their casspirs, their tanks, and their weapons of destruction. Let them pray to that god. Our God is the living God— the God of justice and freedom. To this God we will pray. To his service we will dedicate ourselves.

And so, my people, understand that our struggle is against the evil spirits of this world. Let us remain with Jesus. Let us remain with the Spirit of God in our hearts. Let us depend on his power. Not on the power of guns or the destruction of life. That will be my message to you always. Let us seek the peace which only God himself will give us in this country, even though they who rule so harshly may not understand it. Even today I do not hate them. I will not hate them, but I will resist them until the very end, because I love this country and I love them and I love my people too much to allow the oppressors to destroy us. This we must know.

In our gospel story, the father of the sick boy came to Jesus and explained his dilemma. At the same time, his dilemma became the dilemma of Jesus' disciples, because they could not heal this boy. It was painful. After all, they knew Jesus best, walked with him, heard his voice, understood him better than anyone else. They heard his teachings. And yet they were not able to heal the boy. That was *their* dilemma; a dilemma which became an embarrassment not only before the father, but especially also before the scribes and Pharisees. As our story begins, there was an argument between the scribes and Pharisees and the disciples of Jesus, because the disciples could not heal the boy. They seemed helpless. They had heard Jesus say that if you have faith, you will tell this mountain to move itself from here into the sea. Why couldn't they do it now? They had heard Jesus say that if you have faith even like a mustard seed you will tell this tree to uproot itself and remove itself to another place. Why couldn't they do that? This was their dilemma.

But as Jesus arrives the real nature of the dilemma is revealed. Jesus comes and tells them: "Oh faithless people, how long shall I be with you?" And that, in essence, is the real dilemma of the father and the disciples: their faithlessness, their inability to believe. Jesus says, "All things are possible for those who believe." I smiled a little cynically when I read that the first time. I thought: "God, if this is true, why am I still in this prison? If this is true, why is this government still in government? If this is true, why can they roam our streets and shoot our people while there is nothing we can do about it? If this is true, how is it possible that the church of Jesus Christ cannot stand together? That even in the church we are still divided? Why is it that some in the church are willing to sell our brothers and sisters for the sake of position or out of fear or for love of money? Why? How can I believe that if we only believe *all things* are possible—even the removal of this evil government?" That is possible, if you believe, Jesus says.

But the problem lies not with Jesus, nor with God, nor with the promises of God. The problem lies with us, with you and with me. We are the problem. And in this respect the problem is not even the government of this country with all its power, because God can remove them like I can remove this little piece of paper. And they know it— that's why I was in jail. But the promises of God are clear. We must learn not to be intimidated by the so-called "realities" of our world. Right through the Bible the promises of God are there. "Abraham," said God, "you will have a son. Even though you are so old, you will have a son." And Abraham and Sarah did have a son, for the promises of God endure. Joseph dreams. God promises him in that dream: "I will lift you up, even though you do not count among your brothers, and I will make you one to whom even they will look for help." Joseph is sold by his brothers as a slave. Joseph is thrown in jail by Potiphar and it seems that all is lost. Yet somehow the promises of God remain true, and Joseph is raised up to become the symbol of God's providence not only for Egypt but for the whole world. Mary hears the promise of God that the Messiah will be born and God's new day will dawn. The high and the mighty will be thrown from their thrones. The rich will be sent away empty and the poor will be lifted up from the dust of the earth. The humble will be lifted up and placed in high places by God, and the hungry will be filled with good things. This is the promise of God.

I heard and I believed. I learned to depend, not on Allan Boesak who can talk and argue his way out of anything, but on the promises of God alone. I was humbled before God for almost four weeks. Twenty-five days of solitary confinement, spent in prayer, sometimes fasting, have taught me to depend on the Spirit of God alone, and that the Word of God is true. And as this Word from the gospel came to me then, I said to God: "You will lead me out of here, you will change my situation, you will change this land, you will bring our people our freedom, you will give our people back our dignity, you will give our people vision, you will give our people your love, you will give our people their land, you will give our people the strength to stand, and to believe and to fight, *if I believe*. If I believe, all things are possible."

Today I am here, back in this pulpit not because of *my* faith but because the God of heaven and earth is alive. And I say to you, my people, my own congregation, we have gone through so many difficult times this year, but God has brought us closer together. Keep that love in your hearts. Keep each other in love and in communion of spirit and in communion of commitment. Let the congregation of Bellville become a light and a symbol of love and commitment to Jesus Christ, of love and commitment to the world. Let this church become a symbol of how Christians in this country must participate in this struggle for the sake of Jesus Christ, and also for the sake of justice and peace. Be an example to the Dutch Reformed Mission Church, even to your Moderator. Be an example to every single church. Be an example to every organization. Let the light of Jesus become alive in this congregation, not for our own sakes but for the sake of him who died for us and for the sake of the truth, for the sake of justice, for the sake of peace. Let us challenge the tensions within ourselves. Let us not become cynical. Let us not become hopeless. Let us believe in a committed, faithful, peaceful community. Let us see visions of love and peace and harmony and dignity and liberation for our country, for *all* the people. And all things are possible for those who believe. To believe is to stand up and be counted for Jesus and for justice. To believe is to stand up and to work for justice. To believe is to be willing to take the risks knowing that God is on your side.

I can tell you this now with more conviction than ever before. He who believes, she who believes and works for justice and for peace will never be alone. You will never be alone because Jesus promised that whatever happens, he will never leave us alone. Even in the darkness of a cell in solitary confinement. So let us believe and not despair. Let us believe and work for justice. Let us believe and seek peace. Let us believe and challenge evil in this world. Let us believe and build together a community of love and joy and power and liberation.

There is one last word. If you believe, you can make this your own. Dietrich Bonhoeffer, that courageous German theologian who had so much influence on my life, as much as Martin Luther King had, was killed by the Nazis because of his resistance to their evil. A few weeks before Germany was freed by the allied forces the Germans hanged him. He was only thirty-nine years old. I love that man, and I love his testimony and praise God for him. In January 1935 Bonhoeffer wrote to his brother and said: "There are things in this world which are worth fighting for without any compromise whatsoever. And it seems to me that peace and social justice, which is really Jesus Christ, is such a cause." That is my belief. My people, believe in Jesus Christ and make this your conviction. That is what I told the major when I had read that piece. I told him that again on Thursday when I was told I would be released. I say this to you this morning and to those of the security police who are monitoring this sermon this morning. There are things in this world which are worth standing up for and fighting for without compromise: peace and justice, which is really Jesus Christ.

I believe in Jesus.

I believe in justice.

I believe in peace.

I believe in liberation.

I believe in God's vision for this country.

I believe, also, that it will come true, for Jesus is saying it again to me and to you. Don't worry about my detention or my bail conditions. Don't worry about my trial. God will take care of all of us. I do not worry. I sleep well at night. My life is in the hands of God. God will take care of us. You, you must commit yourselves anew.

Believe in Jesus.

Believe in Jesus and fight for what is right.

God bless you all! Amen.

14

The Price Is High, but the End Is Near

My dear brothers and sisters, my text today comes from the book of Psalms, Psalm 3: "Oh Lord, how many are my foes. Many are rising against me. Many are saying of me, there is no help for him in God. But thou, O Lord, art the shield about me, my glory and the lifter of my head. I cry aloud to the Lord, and he answers me from his holy hill. I lie down and sleep; I wake again, for the Lord sustains me. I am not afraid of ten thousands of people who have set themselves against me round about. Arise, O Lord, deliver me, O my God, for thou dost smite all my enemies on the cheek; thou dost break the teeth of the wicked. Deliverance belongs to the Lord. Thy blessing be upon thy people."

I am grateful today for this opportunity, and for all of you who have come, and for all of you who have participated in the service. I am especially grateful for our brother here who has come today as a symbol of our unity in this community and of the fact that we understand the calling that we have received from God, and that this struggle for justice and for peace and for human liberation is a calling that goes beyond the boundaries of church and religion. I am grateful for your presence here sir.

I am also grateful for Trevor, for we know that the minister's men are looking for him and that they are asking every day how they can find him to detain him and do I don't know what with him in that jail. But he has chosen the occasion of this service to be present today, to say to us that this struggle shall continue.

Those men who put us in jail and who question us and who think up charges in the middle of the night because sleep has fled from their eyes—they cannot sleep. Their consciences bother them because they

---

Allan Boesak preached this sermon on October 6, 1985, shortly after his own release from detention, at a prayer service for political detainees.

know that time is up, and while they cannot sleep they think of charges to put down on paper, and they take us to court in communities across the land. And because they know that they really cannot ban us, because that would look too bad, they make up a banning order in the form of bail conditions and they impose that upon us. And they think that now the voice of justice, the voice of peace, and the voice for liberation has been silenced.

I want to say to them again that it is not my voice that they are trying to silence. They are trying to silence the voice of the Almighty God—and that is not possible. Justice does not belong to human beings to do with what we like. Justice belongs to God, and God gives that justice to a people to be the basis of our struggle, to be the vision into our future, to be the sustenance as the road gets long and difficult and as we get weary. Only God can take that vision away. Only God can take that sustenance away. It is not in the power of a government to take that away from a struggling people. That they must understand.

The government doesn't even have power to give or to share. Mr. P. W. Botha said again the other day, "The government is willing to share its power." With whom? What power do they have to share? Jesus Christ said a long time ago as he stood before Pontius Pilate, "You would have no power over me were it not given you from above." So I say to P. W. Botha and I say to Louis Le Grange, I say to Magnus Malan, and all of those henchmen of Satan who think that they rule this land: "You would have no power over us were it not given you from above. And God has given us a clear sign in this land that power is being taken away from you because you do not deserve it. You have misused it."

But there is something else that I want you to understand today as we meditate in this service upon a question of our own situation and the struggle. Psalm 3 is a psalm that David wrote while he was on the run from his son Absalom. Absalom was planning a military coup. He sat at the gate of the city, speaking to all who would come by, trying to explain to them that he would be a much better king than David. The danger of the situation for David, my brothers and sisters, was clear. We know that in the end he had to flee from Jerusalem across the River Jordan to hide away from his own child. The danger was clear, the situation was serious because it was not only David in his person who was endangered. The reign of David, the throne of David, symbolized something—it represented God's justice in the world and for

Israel. David was the kind of king that God wanted to use as his example of the kind of reign that the Messiah would have in the world. And so what Absalom was trying to undermine was not merely the throne of his father, but the dream of God—justice, love, peace, compassion, and understanding.

So David says twice in the first two verses, "Many are rising up against me; my enemies are too many for me to count." This story is also recounted in the second book of Samuel, chapter 15, where it says that the hearts of the men of Israel were drawn toward Absalom. Verse 2 in the psalm is a cry of pain and anguish from a troubled heart. David says that many are saying of him, "No help is coming to him from God. God has left him in the lurch; God has left him alone. He looks around and there is no one to support him. The power of his enemies is too much for him." It seems in that situation as if even God is not only silent but also powerless over against the power of Absalom and his plans. But then David looks at God and he says, "My faith shall remain. I will be certain that God will help. God shall rise up and save me. Thou dost smite my enemies in the face."

In 2 Samuel we hear that the armies of David go out, they fight against Absalom, Absalom's armies are defeated, and Absalom himself is killed. When David hears the news he goes up into his room, and he refuses to eat. He refuses to drink. He refuses to rejoice. He sees no reason to celebrate his liberation. He has come back from exile, he has crossed the Jordan River once again, he is once again enthroned in Jerusalem. But he is unhappy, and he mourns the death of his son. He grieves so much that the soldiers become restless and even a little ashamed until Joab comes and speaks to him and says, "How can you do this. These men have been willing to give up their lives for you. They have left their wives and their children for you. They have left their homes for you. They have risked everything for you. God has given you victory over your enemies. You have prayed for this victory. Now that God has granted your prayer, what are you doing? You mourn because you now begin to understand that the price of liberation is costly." Then David realizes this is the truth, and he comes out and speaks to his men.

The point, my brothers and sisters, that I want to make today is precisely this. It is not necessary for me today to tell you what is happening in our country; you know that. It is not necessary for me to explain to you what the nature of our struggle for justice and peace and liberation is; you know that. It is not necessary for me to explain to you what your calling is, how clear you must be in your own minds; you know that. Many of you have participated, are participating, in this struggle. Too many of us are still standing on the sidelines, wondering whether we should come in or not; whether it will be safe or not; worrying about our own safety; worrying about our jobs; worrying about Carter Ibrahims; worrying about I don't know who. Many of us have joined this struggle, and that is important.

But we must know that there is a price that we must pay for liberation. This is no joke, this thing that we are engaged in. When people are no longer sure whether they will be there tomorrow, it is no joke. When our children's education is being disrupted, it is no joke. When mothers and fathers will not know whether they will see their children together around the table tonight as they saw them last night and the day before, it is no joke. And when our townships are being overrun by troop carriers and tank-like vehicles and soldiers with guns and live ammunition, it is no joke. And when people are being beaten up and there is no respect for little children or for pregnant women or for our fathers and mothers who have come along in age, this is no joke.

But as this happened, and as the months went on and on, and as the death toll rose, and as many more were picked up and detained, locked up in their jails, and as many more had to go underground in hiding so that they could not continue the work that the people have entrusted them to do—as this was happening and as it seemed as if all of what we were trying to do could not keep the guns away from us and the dogs and the whips and the quirts and the tear gas—as this was happening, many of us started doubting. We asked the questions: What now? Is this really worth it? When will it end? Wasn't this enough? Yes, yes, yes, we are willing to sacrifice, but how much more? I am saying to you who have those feelings in your heart, you are like David. Because as the moment of liberation comes near, so the price that we have to pay for that liberation will become higher and higher and higher.

My brothers and sisters, we are not dealing with some benevolent government who understands justice and mercy and freedom and liberation and compassion. We are not dealing with people who understand the struggle of a people to be free. We are not dealing with people who understand the meaning of the word dignity. We are dealing with people who have closed off their hearts and their minds and their ears so that they cannot hear the voice of God anymore. We are dealing with people whose hearts have so been hardened that they cannot understand the will of God for this country anymore. I have said so in the past, and I will say so again: in this government we are not dealing with the servant of God, we are dealing with the beast from the sea. That is what we are dealing with, and you had better be clear about it.

And as for those men who call themselves Christians, we are not dealing with Christians. We are dealing with people who have long since forgotten what it means to open this Word of God and to hear the voice of God as it speaks to them. That is who we are dealing with.

So I am saying to you that the price we will have to pay is not paid yet. The struggle is not over yet. As I sat in that jail for twenty-five days in solitary confinement and thought at one point I would go out of my mind, I knew that this was not yet the end. There will be many more such moments, either for me or for others. Many more of our people will have to lose their jobs because of their commitment to the struggle for justice. There will be many more like that. There will be many more of our children who will not be able to go to school because of the crisis to which this government has brought us.

Let me say of the crisis we are in today: don't let anybody tell you that this crisis was brought upon us either by our children or by our teachers or by the workers or by the UDF or by the trade unions. Those are the lies and the propaganda without which no unjust government can survive. They have to use them; otherwise they cannot live. But the chaos in this country is the result of the policy of a government which is unjust, cruel, inhuman, un-Christian. It has no relation at all to human dignity and decency. This you must understand. And as long as this government is in power, parents, your children will be in a situation of chaos. As long as this government is in power our society will be in chaos. As long as this government is in power our land will be in chaos.

And so as we fight against this system, remember: the struggle will be long and hard. As we pay the price, don't look around. Don't say, I have had enough; I have prayed enough. Don't say, I have struggled enough. Don't say, I have suffered enough. As long as the blood on the streets which has flown from the bodies of our children is not dry, that blood will call to God in heaven and to you. Don't close your eyes. Don't close your ears. Don't close your heart. It may very well be, my brothers and sisters, that this government will continue to repress us, and I fully expect that it will happen—the repression will grow. The

Carter Ibrahims, and the Louis Le Granges, and the P. W. Bothas of this world will say what they say and do what they do more and more, because the more we struggle and victory comes closer, the more the world sees them for what they are. The more we rise up with dignity and power to challenge the unjust powers, the more they will have to shout, the more they will have to shoot, the more they will have to kill. It is true; they will do that. Apartheid is like that god Molech that lived on the sacrifice of little children in the ancient days. As long as that beast is alive, we will have to make sacrifices.

But I am telling you now, we are seeing the final convulsion of that peace. And as David learned, you must learn: there is no easy way to freedom. There is no golden road to freedom. There is no rosy road to freedom—forget about that. I am saying to you that our calling is clear. Our goal is clear. The struggle must continue at every level because the end is near. The South African government knows—but I will say it to them again today so that they will understand it and you must know it—their end is near. I mean their end is near!

And so we will remain faithful to God, faithful to our calling, faithful to our faith. We will pay the price, but the end is near. We hear the voices of anguish and pain. We hear them, and the price is high, but the end is near. We see the suffering of mothers and fathers and children, and the price is high, but the end is near. We see the disruption of our communities and we see the chaos in which we live, and the price is high, but the end is near. We see the tears on the cheeks of those who have buried loved ones who have died in the struggle, and we share their grief. And we know the price is high, but the end is near. We see at this moment justice still stumbling on the streets of South Africa and apartheid still reigning supreme on the throne of this land, and the price is high, but the end is near. We hear the voice of the beast as it shouts at us, as it tries to frighten us, as it tries to intimidate us, and we know the price is high, but the end is near.

We know, we know that we will have to pay, and it is costly. And the struggle is long and hard, and the road is arduous. The price is high, but the end is near. Do not despair. Do not look around. Do not betray our faith. Do not betray our children. Do not betray our fathers. Do not betray our mothers. Do not betray our vision. Do not betray the justice we are fighting for. Do not betray the land. We will see that it will rise up out of the ashes of this country as apartheid will crumble to dust. The price will be high, but the end is near.

15

I Have Seen Satan Fall

My dear brothers and sisters, there are very few people assembled from the townships here this morning, and we know why. As we continue our service let us pray to God that he will protect our brothers and sisters who were on their way to this service and who in all probability have been stopped this morning by the police at roadblocks. We do not know what is happening to them, but in the midst of all that terror may God be with them and may God protect them.

I must say something else before I begin my sermon. You have all seen in the newspapers the explanation of what the state of emergency means. You also may have seen the definition of what is called subversion. I am already in a court case, having been accused of subversion. If you have read that definition clearly you understand that it actually means that anything you say that somehow criticizes the government, or that criticizes the actions of the minister for law and order, or that criticizes the actions of his police and army, or anything that can be understood by him to be subversive—that is an offense, punishable by law.

Now you know me—I'm not a very brave person. But I must say to the minister this morning—and I know that he is listening—that if in the course of this sermon, in preaching the Word of God, I say something that disturbs you, Mr. Minister, or Mr. President, or whoever else makes decisions of life and death over our people; if in the course of this sermon I say something that you think is subversive; if in the course of this sermon I say something that you feel is criticism and therefore an offense; if you think that I say something that I should not say, please go ahead and think so. Because when you are called to preach the gospel of Jesus Christ you cannot turn around and search out what the government finds acceptable. You will have to say what God wants you

---

June 16, 1986, marked the tenth anniversary of the Soweto uprising. The ceremonies and demonstrations commemorating that day were the focus of international attention, and at their center was this sermon Allan Boesak preached at a memorial service in Cape Town.

to say, and that Word shall be forever the last Word. No one gladly confronts this evil government. No one gladly goes to jail—I've been there and know what it's like. But if for the preaching of this Word I have to go again, then so be it.

One never says these things lightly, my brothers and sisters. You know that. We have a government in this country that we have not chosen—but certainly God has not chosen people who have placed themselves in power and who keep themselves in power by using the most incredible violence against our defenseless people. We know what they are capable of doing, and so it is not as if we are here trying to defy them. But I would rather defy the South African government, and I would rather anger Mr. Louis Le Grange and his wards of—wild beasts, I almost said—than risk the great sin of being disobedient to my God.

So this morning we have chosen for our text what you read in Luke, chapter 10, verse 18: "And Jesus said to them, 'I saw Satan fall like lightning from heaven.' " I saw Satan fall like lightning from heaven. We are here to commemorate Soweto 1976, to think again upon that most solemn moment in our history. We know what June 16 means for us. It means that after almost a generation of passivity, it was our children who rose up and said no to apartheid, to continued exploitation, to inferior and unequal education; no to racism and oppression. And at the same time they said yes to dignity, freedom, and the future for all the children of this land. We know that Soweto is more than just a name. It is more than just a symbol. We know that Soweto has become the perpetual condition of South Africa. We know that the words from Shakespeare's play *Macbeth* have become so true for our country during this time: "Alas, for a country almost afraid to know itself; it cannot be called our mother, but our grave." South Africa has become a grave for the hopes of millions of oppressed people. It has become the grave for the dreams of our children, their dreams of freedom and hope and joy. It has become to a large extent the grave of the authenticity of the gospel of Jesus Christ, that gospel that has been so evilly abused by those in power who call themselves Christians, while every single act they commit is a denial of this God they claim to know and serve. It has become the grave of the dreams of those of us who hold on to dignity and to life and to a future.

During Soweto 1976 our people forever lost their innocence. We then saw our children going into the streets with nothing in their hands but placards calling for the removal of Afrikaans—such a simple, simple issue—from their curriculum. That's how it began. They went into the streets, when others were detained, saying we do not want to make war, we simply want you to release our friends. And later on we saw them on the street battling the police armed with R-1 rifles, they with nothing in their hands, singing freedom songs and dying on the streets. We then saw how Hector Peterson was killed, the first boy to die in that new era of violence and oppression and hatred and cruelty. We saw the extent the South African government is willing to go in order to defend white privilege and their own position of power. We saw then that they are willing to kill our children by the hundreds, only so they can cling to power. We saw then that violence was going to be the language of the South African government from that time on—as it had been before, but even more so from that moment. We then knew what it is, finally and clearly, that we are dealing with.

Now they have again, for the second time in one year, declared a state of emergency. They have banned all these commemorations. They first tried to ban our church services, but when the church of Jesus Christ said very clearly, "You can try to ban these services; we will continue anyway," then they had to backpedal on that one. And yet yesterday they arrested a whole churchful of people at St. Nicholas. They broke up the service with tear gas, and policemen with guns took them away, the women to one jail, the men elsewhere—even children gone with their mothers. Fourteen days they will be locked up. Their crime: having come together on a Sunday afternoon in a parish church to listen to the Word of God and to pray.

They do this, brothers and sisters, because they want to force us to forget June 16, 1976. They want to force us to forget the history of this country, the history of our struggle. They have robbed us of our land. They have oppressed our people. They have raped our country. They have undermined our faith. They have vilified and exiled and jailed and killed our leaders. They have terrorized our people in our communities. They have massacred our children. And now they want us to forget. We shall never forget. We shall never annul this part of our history, simply to let it fade away or to be forced out of our minds because they want us to be so fearful of them that we become a people without a past. The government knew too well that our commemoration would be once again a national demonstration of our rejection of its policies, of its force, of its undemocratic rule, of its very legitimacy.

They knew that. And we are here not because in the first place we are looking for confrontation, as they so glibly lie on their television. We are here not because we want to die, but we are here because we refuse to let our fear become the grave of our dignity. And it is time that the South African government understands that.

How can we forget June 16? How can we forget what we have seen since then, because since then, June 16, Soweto has been enacted over and over and over again in our country's history. The story of Hector Peterson and all those other children has been multiplied a thousand-fold, in Soweto and in townships right across South Africa. You know that. Since then we have heard the horrifying story of the efforts of this government completely to obliterate from the face of this country the presence of our people, or at least the kind of presence that we want to be, namely, a dignified, protesting, hopeful, accusing presence. As long as we are here and as long as we rise up and as long as we remind ourselves of what we have been and of what we shall become, as long as we remind ourselves of the promises of God, that very presence will be an accusation at the address of the South African government. It will be an unmasking act; it will be an exposure of what they are.

Since then we have heard of children of three years and five years and six years old, brutally murdered. Since then we have heard of Bernard Fortuin and others like him who had to die on the streets of Cape Town and elsewhere. Since then we have seen the children of Crossroads. We have seen incredible criminal acts played out right in front of our eyes.

We cannot forget because we are the church. We are the body of Jesus Christ. And as long as these things happen, we know that the body of Christ is being broken every single day. As long as these things happen, Christ is again persecuted, denied, and crucified. We are the church and we are called to preach the gospel of Jesus Christ, a gospel of hope and liberation, but also a gospel of judgment. And we must not be afraid to do that. We are the church and we are called in this world to recognize the reality of evil. We are called to recognize the presence of the devil in the midst of our history.

Because you see—we have said it before and we must say it again—evil is real. We must not make the mistake of thinking that Satan is merely a figment of someone's imagination or that Satan is no more than some nightclub comedian—usually painted with two little horns, usually black, usually with a long tail sticking out from somewhere.

And we smile because we sophisticated people of the modern world cannot believe in that anymore. I am telling you, please don't make that mistake, for Satan is alive. Satan is real. Satan is what he has always been—an adversary. He is the enemy of God and of God's people. He is a destroyer of peace and of all that is good. He is a liar and a deceiver. He is an accuser of God's children. That is what the Bible calls him, and the Bible speaks in graphic terms about the reality of evil and about the presence of Satan among God's people.

Satan is real. He does not and cannot abide love and peace and justice. He elevates propaganda and lies to the level of truth. He is real, and you see him on television trying to explain what the state of emergency means and why it was necessary. Satan is real, and from now on he will be the only one making press statements and explaining what has happened to people, because the press will not be allowed to be there. Satan is real, and he is alive and he has decided that he will let loose his roaring lions. They are out to devour all that they can find and no one will be able to say, "This is what has happened," because he has decided who will speak on whose behalf. And these independent witnesses that you see in front of you will not be allowed to show to the world what Satan is doing. He is doing it, but no one must know. And so all the people in Britain and in Europe and in the United States who hear will not hear what is really happening, but only what he has decided that they will hear.

Satan is real and sometimes he is in the pulpit justifying the oppression of our people, telling our people—our people—that their oppression is somehow the will of God and there is nothing that we can do about it. When you are oppressed, don't worry about it; it's God's will. And when you are thrown in jail, don't worry about it; it's God's will. And when they take away your homes, don't worry about it; it's God's will. And when they detain you with your children, it's God's will, and when they burn down your shacks in Crossroads, it's God's will, and when they kill you on the streets, it's God's will. Satan is on the pulpit telling people that sometimes.

But we know that that is a lie. It is not God's will that our people should live the way we do. It is not God's will that we should have a government that understands nothing about justice and truth and freedom and dignity and humanity. It is not God's will that we suffer so. It is not God's will that Crossroads is what it is today. It is not God's will that a mother with a four-month-old baby and a six-year-old hand-

icapped boy should be burned down in a shack while people stand by
in their uniforms and do nothing about it. It is not God's will. God's
will is for justice and for peace and for freedom and for dignity and for
love and for genuine reconciliation.

And that's why I'm telling you, Satan is real. Right now he has an
order that says he can go around killing our people on the streets, and
then he stands up in parliament justifying the murderers of our children.
Don't you tell me that the devil is not real. Don't you try to deceive
yourself by making as if he is not real. Recognize him for what he is.
Know what we are dealing with at this stage of South Africa's history.
We have arrived at one of the most difficult moments in our history.
Already we are standing knee-deep in blood. The South African government is—I have said this before—no longer a servant of God, but
the beast from the sea, seeking whom it can devour. Our people are
pushed relentlessly into more and more and more violence. We can see
it, and we can no longer speak simply of a peaceful solution to our
problems—not when our people are dying, when we are dying.

You know how our efforts for nonviolent change have all ended in
massacres over the years: 1960 in Sharpeville, 1976 in Soweto, 1980
in Cape Town, and from 1983 onward. In 1985 we called together a
march, a nonviolent, peaceful march, simply to give a message to Nelson Mandela and to the world that he and others should be free and
that South Africa should begin to understand the realities of our situation. We did not have a single gun; we did not intend to look for one.
We did not have a single stone; we did not intend to throw even one.
And yet while I was in Pretoria maximum security prison and you went
to the stadium for your peaceful demonstration, they came with their
tear gas and their dogs and their guns and their bullets.

And still this is not enough. Our people are sometimes on the brink
of despair. What else should we do? How else shall we show our
protest? How else shall we give embodiment to our hope? How else
shall we continue our struggle when all peaceful protests have been
made impossible by this government, which then turns around and, with
unbelievable hypocrisy, says that other people must first denounce violence so that we can all talk together?

In the meantime Britain and the United States continue to be the
main supporters of this South African government. They continue to
find excuses for this government. There is not enough reason, Britain
says, to act. And the United States can only say that all sides must

show restraint. For God's sake, Mr. Reagan, what restraint must we show more than we have shown? Who are the people today, on this June 16, who are walking around with guns and rifles and live ammunition? Who are the people who did so ten years ago? Who are the people who have done so consistently almost every day for the last ten years? What restraint must we show? How many white people have died at our hands, Mr. Reagan? During the last ten years, how many white children have we shot, have we killed, have we locked up, have we tortured? What restraint are you talking about, Mr. Reagan? I cannot begin to understand this hypocrisy. We are an unarmed people. The restraint Mr. Reagan is asking of us is not to restrain from violence, but to restrain and refrain from protesting. He wants us to accept this evil that is being done to our people. If this is what you ask, Mr. President of the United States, please go and ask it elsewhere. We cannot give that to you.

Ronald Reagan and Margaret Thatcher know this: if the situation were reversed today, if Nelson Mandela were sitting in Pretoria and P. W. Botha in Robben Island, if white children were massacred on the street as black children are today, Ronald Reagan and Margaret Thatcher would have acted a long time ago. They would not have waited. Ronald Reagan knows he would have sent in his troops under some excuse, and he would have helped white South Africa in such a battle.

But it is because we are not white, my people, that this is happening. It is because your children's lives do not count in the eyes of Mr. Reagan and Mrs. Thatcher. I have never thought that the day would come that I would have to say this from a public pulpit, but I am saying it now. Maybe there is nothing we can do about the United States of America, and maybe there is no way we can speak to the hearts of the people of Britain, but there is one thing that they must know. We are a people, weak as we are in terms of their understanding of power, weak as we are in terms of their military might and the military might of their friends in Pretoria, we are a people determined to be free. And there is nothing that they can do that will ever break the spirit of our people. There is nothing that they can do that will turn this tide of resistance. There is nothing that they can do that will turn us away from our goal. We have kept our feet on this course and we will walk it. We have seen the goal ahead and we will reach it. There is a fire that we have lit in our heart and it burns for freedom. It will not go out, and they must understand that.

No, my people, I do not know what to say to you anymore. For years now you have listened to me from pulpits and platforms, and you have heard me plead for our nonviolent resistance because I believe that that is the best way. That is the way of peace. You have heeded those calls, and you have come unarmed when we have called; we have participated in those actions, and you have responded, and you—and you today bear the scars of that action. So no one today in South Africa can simply call for nonviolent response. And yet I must plead with you. Somehow we must remember that the dream of God is one of peace and humanity. War and hatred and destruction is not God's will. I can no longer simply judge people who choose the path of violence, but I must say to you, beware of what we do when we do it not merely for the sake of our just cause, but out of our anger and despair. I know I can no longer demand; I am simply asking and pleading in the midst of a situation that has already become too much for us to bear.

Let us also remember what Jesus says: "I have seen Satan fall like lightning from heaven." He does not say that I hope to see Satan fall. He does not say I think Satan will fall. He does not say I will call together a commission of inquiry and they will look into the possibility of Satan's falling. He says, "I have seen Satan fall." That means that the power of Satan has already been broken. There are people who think that the declaration of a state of emergency is a sign of power on the side of the South African government. It is not. It is a sign of blind panic. It is a sign of desperation. It is a sign of their powerlessness. Violence is never a sign of power. Violence and hatred are never signs of how strong you are. It shows unashamedly the weaknesses of the oppressor. They have nothing else *but* violence. They have nothing else *but* theft. They have nothing else *but* murder and more senseless murder.

The state president in his speech the other day said a lot of things that we cannot go into now, but one thing he said that I cannot simply ignore is this. He said, "South Africa is quite alone now in the world," or something to that effect. "We only have," he says, "our forces to help us and our God." Now, he may have his forces to help him; that I will grant him. South Africa may be producing more guns than ever before; that I will grant him. They may have flown forty thousand more troops into Cape Town; that I will grant him. They may have powerful friends in the West; that I will grant him.

But what I cannot grant him is his bland assertion that they have God. Mr. President, let me tell you clearly: the God you are talking

about is not the God of the Bible. Woe to you, South African government, for your god is an idol. Your god is racism. Your god is oppression. Your god is guns and dogs and bullets. Your god has to be carried
because he cannot walk. He has ears but he cannot hear. He has hands
but he cannot help you. And in the end you will sit with all your gods
surrounding you and you will be destroyed. Woe to you, South African
government, for your life will end like the life of Pharaoh. Your life
will end like the life of Ahab. Your life will end like the life of Jezebel.
It is not I that say so; it is the Bible that says so.

So if you want to throw us in jail, do so. But don't think that you
are doing it in the name of the God who is the Father of Jesus Christ.
If you want to destroy our communities, do so. But don't do it in the
name of the God who is the Father of Jesus Christ. If you want to
torture us in your prisons, do so. But don't think you can do it in the
name of the God who is the God of liberation and the God of Israel
and the God of his people. If you want to kill us, do so. But don't think
that you can do that in the name of the God of the Bible, for that God
will rise up and that God will judge you for what you are. And that
God will exact from you his just wage. That God will destroy all evil,
including the evil of this government. Of that I am sure.

For Jesus has said, "I have seen Satan fall." Satan may be riding
high today; Jesus says, "I have seen Satan fall." Satan may be getting
his guns ready today; Jesus says, "I have seen Satan fall." And even as
the troops converge upon us, I have seen Satan fall. And even as you
glibly lie on your television and tell the world what is not happening
and take your lies and make them into truth, I have seen Satan fall.
Even as the tears will again blind the eyes of all our mothers, I have
seen Satan fall. And even though these prison doors shut behind us a
hundred times, I have seen Satan fall. And even as our blood continues
to flow, I have seen Satan fall.

Do not despair, my people. This is not the final chapter. For them
yes, but not for us. Do not despair, my people. Their guns will not have
the last word. Do not despair, my people. We are marching on to
victory, and they know it. That is why they are doing what they are
doing. Do not give up now. Let not fear overcome your hearts. Let not
despair drive you into the wilderness of desperation. Do not turn your
back now on the graves of our children. Fight on. Believe on. Struggle
on. The moment is dark now, but the sun shall surely rise. The night